A Beautiful Resistance

The Fire Is Here

Copyright, Gods & Radicals, 2016.
Most rights reserved,
Duplication or distribution for commercial purposes forbidden.
Authors, photographers and artists retain primary rights —
contact Gods & Radicals for creator queries.

Individual articles may be quoted with attribution.

First Printing, 2016.

Direct all queries to
Editor, Gods & Radicals
Editor@godsandradicals.org

copyedited by Cat Mead, Lia Hunter and Rhyd Wildermuth

Gratitude
Foreword: *Emma Restall Orr* - 1
Introduction: *Lorna Smithers* - 3

IGNITE
This Craft Is Not For Your Consumption: *Mandrake* - 8
"everything breathes the revolutionary spirit": *Nina George* - 10

THE SICKNESS AND THE MEDICINE
Deconstructing Local Mythologies: *Alley Valkyrie* - 14
The Year of the Black Lake: *Lauren Lockhart* - 19
The Dangers Facing Seneca Lake: *Joe DiCicco* - 20
Song of the swollen cells: *Nimue Brown* - 23
Only Connect: *Yvonne Aburrow* - 25
We Are Living on Turtle Island: *Pegi Eyers* - 30
Windsong: *Lia Hunter* - 35

SOVEREIGNTY AND THE TRIALS OF LOVE
Love and Possession of the Land: *Heron* - 38
Eriu Addresses the False Kings: *Geraldine Moorkens Byrne* - 43
Giving Power, Taking Power: *Sophia Burns* - 44
All Hail the Runners: *Hunter Hall* - 47
We Are the Rude: *Rhyd Wildermuth* - 49
love letter / carta de amor: *Simcha Bensefis* - 62

A Forest Allegiance

Woman of the Sap: *Nicolas Guy Williams* - 65
Plant Magic: *Sean Donahue* - 66
The Wood at the World's End: *William A. Young & Hanne T. Fisker* - 69
Myrddin's Scribe: *Lorna Smithers* - 78
Wonder is a weapon, too: *Gordon MacLellan* - 80
Of Worlding: *Kadmus* - 83
Scrolls: *Catriona McDonald* - 87

Footsteps In The Embers

The Sui Generis Sermon: *Dr Bones* - 90
The Fire is Here: *Heathen Chinese* - 95
Bataille and the Dead: *Finnchuill* - 104
Millennium: *Christopher Scott Thompson* - 120

About the Artists - 112

Works Cited - 114

Our Deepest Thanks

We'd like to thank the following incredible people for their financial support of our work.

Alkistis Dimech & Peter Grey of Scarlet Imprint
Jessica Minah
Jeffrey Keefer
Matt Dyer
Ryan M. McGrath
Sharon Bourke
Casandra Johns
David Dashifen Kees
Andrew M. Reichart
Chris Richards
HopeGraceFury

Foreword

Emma Restall Orr

When asked to write the foreword to this collection, my eyes skipped over the digital page, avidly drawn to the one word that shone out like a beacon: *anti-capitalism*. Before I'd had a chance to think, I had replied with a yes. With so much of our human population seemingly drugged by the notion of capitalism as not just good, but a global saviour, I see its antithesis as one of the crux words of our time.

With its root in the ancient word *kaput* (meaning head), it stands as the opposable thumb in a fistful of c words that must now be rigorously challenged. That fist's intrusive four fingers – civilisation, colonialism, consumerism and conservatism – are all led by capitalism.

Capitalism isn't about having resources. What makes a capitalist is a person's acute sense of the importance of what they have, and the need to affirm and assert that importance. Hard-headed, counting, weighing and measuring, the capitalist is the one who has, who wants more, and will fight to get it and keep it. Expressed through a nation, a government, a company, a community, a family, aggrandised by the belief in the power of their capital, the capitalist becomes the bully. And he or she is a head case, the force that pushes nature to the point of the unsustainable and unstable. This is the bully we must find the courage to address.

How is the question.

The beauty in this publication's title is inspiring. For raw indignation is graceless. It is a childish objection to a person or situation that has threatened our position, and as such it is just another expression of capital: it is all about me and my sense of self. Equally, the current tendency in Western culture to glorify the victim, to declare one's own state of victimhood and assign culpability, is just as ugly. It is another dualist reaction to the bully, an impulse to fight right back, even if that is through the wailing of the *oh I'm the most wounded, or the most unfairly treated*. The instinct is to amass an opposing stock of capital, or self-importance: pity.

Having dismissed the binary and reactive though, resistance can be truly beautiful. I perceive it as most fruitfully so when it comes with the acceptance of personal responsibility, responsibility for our own behaviour, and for the part we play in every community and ecosystem that our every act of living affects. That is not about capital, about who has a head start, or is a head above whom. It isn't about who is more important, with more dollars in the bank, more followers in the blogosphere, or more troubles to endure. It is not about the me at all. It is about relationship.

When the human world in which we live seems so thick with injustice, it is easy to dummy-spit with outrage. But more often than not, in doing so we rail at some abstract notion of humanity: an organisation or corporation, a government, or even a theory or attitude. Yelling at an individual, it is often not the human being but the role we believe they play in our lives that has provoked our anger. This is not relationship. We have accepted or assumed some human authority, and we are reacting against it. We

THE FIRE IS HERE

bitterly resent the man, and we kick out at him in rage.

But such assaults are often, at best, useless. At worst, clumsily misdirected, they can wound as collateral damage the ordinary people who get in the way. Such blind fights don't touch the individual human beings who are using the power of their capital to cause harm. Indeed, often such actions only toughen the individual capitalist who reinforces his or her defences with an ever widening wasteland.

True relationships are person to person. For when individual human beings come together, to talk, to listen, to learn, to share, to listen and talk, to learn and share, that listening-learning-talking-sharing is the greatest weapon against capitalism that we have.

It doesn't matter whom we know. It matters that we listen, carefully, respectfully, without self-importance, and that we learn from every interaction, and that we share what we learn with others, and make decisions that are wakeful and informed, so that the impact of those decisions causes the least unnecessary harm. The fabric of the human mind, the collective whole of humanity, is a network of individuals. It is said that we are just seven links away from every other human being. We can break through ignorance together, learn together, eat together, we can raise each other up, or we can drag each other down. We are responsible for what we do.

That standpoint works in a secular context, but my perspective is founded on an animistic metaphysics, guided by the pantheism which that entails, and fuelled by the innumerable gods. Accepting that every aspect of nature is experiencing and responding through its own kind of consciousness means that *every* interaction is subject to subject. There are no mindless 'things'. Thus the hierarchies inherent within capitalism dissolve. With decisions made on the basis of equality, capitalism, based on who asserts the power to be a-head, is disarmed.

Many neoPagan traditions promote and celebrate individualism, but distinguishing between individual freedom and individual importance is essential. Freedom, from oneself and from others, to be at one within the greater mind of nature, allows for the wonderful heterogeneity of our world, and that is not just something to celebrate: it is a rich seam of learning.

The diversity of perspectives expressed and images evoked by the writers in this collection makes it well worth immersing oneself in each and every page. Some ideas here I agree with wholeheartedly, some stride right past me, and some leave me befuddled, but each one is an opportunity to listen and learn, that we might strengthen (and make more beautiful) our position as part of the now-crucial resistance.

Emma Restall Orr

Emma Restall Orr is an English animist, anarchist and mystic, ever challenging the complacency of the Western mind, author of the pagan ethics Living with Honour, *the animist metaphysics* The Wakeful World, *and other texts.*

Introduction

Lorna Smithers

I.

'I hunted out and stored in fennel stalk the stolen source of fire that has proved a teacher to mortals in every art and a means to mighty ends. Such is the offence for which I pay the penalty, riveted in fetters beneath the open sky.'
  Aeschylus, *Prometheus Bound*

'Each of them has the care of the fire for a single night in turn, and, on the evening before the twentieth night, the last nun, having heaped wood upon the fire, says, "Brigit, take charge of your own fire ; for this night belongs to you."'
  Gerald of Wales, *The Topography of Ireland*

A stolen fire passed down by generations.

We are the flame-keepers of a questionable heritage.

In many cultures fire is taken from the gods and gifted to mankind by a trickster, who suffers for their hubris, or is kept alive by a group of virgins serving a goddess. These are the costs and vetoes of fire.

Fire, of itself, is amoral. It lights and heats our homes. It burns in the furnaces of factories and power stations and burns them down. It inspires revolutions and burns martyrs. It burned the victims of the Holocaust.

The uses we make of fire are our responsibility. When we look back at its misuses we are suffocated by horror, fettered by sky gods as eagles descend to peck upon our guilty livers.

However, we remember Prometheus was unbound. The unfastening of fetters is a Herculean task. By learning to listen to voices consigned to the flames, walking through fire and awakening to uncomfortable truths, gifting back to the gods ("fire... belongs to you") we can become good flame-keepers.

II.

'Svasud is the name of the father of Summer. He is a man so content that from his name comes the expression 'it is svaslight' referring to what is pleasant. The father of Winter is alternately called Vindloni or Vindsval (Wind Chill). His is the son of Vasad (Damp Cold). These are cruel and cold-hearted kinsmen and Winter takes its nature from them.'
  Snorri Sturluson, *The Prose Edda*

'there was to be battle between Gwyn and Gwythyr every May Day until Judgement Day, and the one that triumphed on Judgement Day would take the maiden.'
  Sioned Davies, *The Mabinogion*

Eternal Summer is founded on the death of Winter.

For thousands of years we have been stealing fuel for our fire from the underworld: the bones and breath of dead worlds.

The smog-blackened chimneys of mill towns, the concrete towers of coal-fired power stations, a million million vehicles chugging on oil have together contributed to the asphyxiating build-up of gases that may postpone the next Ice Age.

Glaciers are calving. Sea levels rising. Last winter in northern England heavy rain caused rivers to burst their banks, washing away venerable old trees and an historic pub, flooding towns and cities and leaving hundreds of people bereft of belongings. This summer is set to be the hottest on record again.

The dialectic between summer and winter is rep-

THE FIRE IS HERE

resented by the battle between two gods: Summer and Winter Kings, and their courtship of the sovereign goddess of the land.

On May Day Summer's King wins and takes the goddess' hand in sacred marriage. Winter's King dies and retreats. He returns for his beloved at summer's end. But for how long?

If either King keeps her forever it will bring about the end of the world.

III.

'Whoever until this day emerges victorious, marches in the triumphal procession in which today's rulers tread over those who are sprawled underfoot. The spoils are, as was ever the case, carried along in the triumphal procession. They are known as the cultural heritage. In the historical materialist they have to reckon with a distanced observer. For what he surveys as the cultural heritage is part and parcel of a lineage which he cannot contemplate without horror.'

Walter Benjamin, *Theses on the Philosophy of History*

'It is dangerous, that power. It is most perilous. It must follow knowledge, and serve need. To light a candle is to cast a shadow.'
Ursula Le Guin, *A Wizard of Earthsea*

Our heritage is as questionable as the stolen fire in which it was forged.

It has taken two devastating world wars, and the dedicated effort of thinkers such as Walter Benjamin, to put into question the ideal of progress which drove the industrial revolution and gave rise to dehumanising and militant right and left-wing ideologies.

Benjamin died of an overdose fleeing the Nazis at Portbou. His *Theses on the Philosophy of History* were passed on to his colleague, Theodor Adorno, by Hannah Arendt. Another manuscript, which some scholars have speculated may have been his completed *Arcades Project*, was forever lost.

The transmission of our heritage and connection with our ancestors are fragile and fraught with danger. They run beyond paganism into interconnectedness with all humanity.

When we look into the flames of a fire we see what collectively we share with the rest of the world: a shared history, a shared responsibility.

The shadow cast by that fire will never go out.

It reminds us as pagans, magic-workers, devotees of our gods, of the need to sustain the fire of love for each other and our seared earth.

On May Eve we gather around the fire in love. We hold hands in the darkness.
We are flame-keepers of a stolen fire brought at great cost.
The fire is here.
Use it wisely.

The Fire Is Here is the work of 26 writers, 5 artists and 2 photographers. The narrative flickered into life as the contributions arranged themselves into a tapestry bound together by summer's burning thread. Taking the form of a Beltane / May Day rite it crackled and roared.

The first section **IGNITE**s the Bel fire and calls in the revolutionary spirit. **THE SICKNESS AND THE MEDICINE** forms a journey of purification where the ills of capitalism are exposed and cures are found at its ailing core. **SOVEREIGNTY AND THE TRIALS OF LOVE** focuses on relationship with the land, gods, and each other and gives voice to the tribulations and joys of love. The spirits of the greenwood offer **A FOREST ALLEGIANCE** and lead to the storytellers' grove. With fire in our heads we confront our social and political situation and depart with revolutionary ancestors leaving **FOOTSTEPS IN THE EMBERS**.

The title *The Fire Is Here* is borrowed from the title of an inspired piece in the journal by Heathen Chinese. My introduction was born from meditating on Li Pallas' stunning cover art. The layout and design have also been completed by Li. I was thrilled when Emma Restall Orr agreed to write the foreword and more so when I read her thought-provoking words.

It has been a pleasure and honour to bring together these thoughts and visions as an act of service to the authors and their lands and deities. To witness pagans from all paths coming together in resistance to capitalism 'to create the world we want now'[1].

As a way of introducing the individual pieces, as an awenydd and poet, I have chosen to compose a cento. This is a poetic form crafted from the words of others. For the artworks I have used a combination of titles and personal impressions.

> We are the flame-keepers of a stolen fire brought at great cost.

[1] In *A Beautiful Resistance #1: Everything We Already Are* (Gods & Radicals, 2015), Rhyd Wildermuth issued the challenge of creating 'the world we want now' in his essay 'An Apparently Impossible Problem' p116

THE FIRE IS HERE

These words are a spellbreaking,
a subterranean fire.
In the valley of sickness
we are healed by what can end us
six hundred feet deep
raise the tainted cup
in the soul of every man.
Only connect! A bond in blood.
We are living on Turtle Island.
The ancient new seductive healing sound
clothed in enchantment
myth and folklore
addresses the False Kings.
The Mother of the Gods answers
"My body is not acreage
savage, immoral, uncivilised, wild,
Earth Mound Mother, Sustain-her of Life.
Come voice yourselves
from tree heart to tree top
in revolutionary magic
shake up the sanity of everyday life
in the Holy Grove
pen roaring and bloody words
trembling and flooded with moonlight.
Tell stories in the summertime.
Hold close the fire until it burns your mind."
The magic-wielders are waking up.
Soulfood for imagination
the fire is already here.
The dead wait for us who are willing to cross
then heal. Then build. Then sing.

As Summer's King triumphs I go to mourn the death of my god.
May the gifts of this journal fire your inspiration
and guide you through the wakening wood.

A BEAUTIFUL RESISTANCE

IGNITE

THIS CRAFT IS NOT FOR YOUR CONSUMPTION
Mandrake

These words are a spell-breaking.
These words are a cutting of energetic ties to spiritual opportunists.
These words are a banishment of the spirit of Capitalism from this circle.
These words are a hex upon over-consumption and unsustainability.
These words are an exorcism of exploitation.
These words are a reclaiming of power and magic.

With these words, freed are all artists and witches, activists and clergy, creators and agitators.
With these words, freed are all who speak them.

This Craft is not for your consumption.
It cannot be reproduced in a factory, sweatshop, boardroom or industrial farm.
This Craft is not entertainment, edutainment, or infotainment.
It will not be performed on command.
This Craft is not a petting zoo.
It is wild with teeth and claws and it may bite off your fingers if you put them near its mouth.
This Craft is not a perfume.
It will not camouflage the stink of your rotting life, your living dead existence.
This Craft is not suitable for general audiences.
It may shock, disturb, or bore you to sleep.
There is no recipe, no pattern, no instruction manual for this Craft.
This Craft is not a shirt you can borrow because you think it would totally look cute on you.
This Craft is not the neatly manicured, perfectly synchronized movement of rehearsed performance over staged props.
You do not see a sign on this Craft that reads "For Sale".
You will not find this Craft on the menu.
This Craft does not come with a guarantee, a warranty, or an insurance policy.
There are no Five Steps to… or 21 Signs That…
There is no like button, no comments box, and no way for you to share this Craft with your friends.

This Craft cannot be put in a box, pulled out every month and a half, and then stuffed back into the box until the next lifeless Sabbat rolls around.

This Craft will not be placed on a shelf or on a pedestal or in a corner.

This Craft is as much me as the blood carrying life through my veins.

Is as much all of humanity as the shared mitochondria in our cells.

Is as much the world as the turning of the seasons, as life, as death, as birth and rebirth.

Is as much the Universe as the dance of the stars and planets, the movement of the tides in sync with the Moon.

This Craft is me: Spirit crawling out of the void on the tenuous thread of heartbeat.

And as much as this Craft longs to connect-

To mix with other magic-

To dance with other spirits-

To burn with collective fire-

To celebrate together the ecstasy of our becoming...

This Craft,

Witchcraft,

My witchcraft is not for you.

You'll have to make your own.

Mandrake

Mandrake is a High Priestess and Witch in the NorthStar tradition of Wicca, and a member of Baltimore Reclaiming. When she isn't in the kitchen or acupuncture clinic, you will find her playing outside in the urban wilderness, puttering in the garden, talking with the tarot, making music, or writing, of course. Her blog can be found at http://theluckystone.co.

"EVERYTHING BREATHES THE REVOLUTIONARY SPIRIT"

Nina George

"The day will come when our silence will be more powerful than the voices
you are throttling today."
—August Spies

November 11th 1887. 4 men are hanged in Chicago. August Spies (pronounced owgust shpees), Albert Parsons, Adolph Fischer, George Engel.

All of the men die stoically, some defiantly. The state makes sure they die slowly, noosed and then strangled. No breaking of necks for a humane exit for them.

Another 2 men are serving life in prison. Samuel Fielden and Michael Schwab (pronounced shvab). 1 man, 15 years. Oscar Neebe.

Another has committed suicide in his cell, dying a slow death from exploding dynamite in his mouth. Louis Lingg.

All this for what heinous crime? For being visible in a movement for an 8-hour working day…

In the late 18th century, many Europeans flocked to the United States seeking work in the land of opportunity. What they found was that pay and conditions were worse than back home. Consequently, they organised. Some agitated. Unions, socialists and anarchists built an uneasy alliance. There were many issues but all came together in the movement for an 8 hour day in a time where 14 to 18-hour days were not uncommon. They called for balance, "8 hours for work – 8 for rest – and 8 for what we will".

On May 4th, 1886, a rally was convened as a response to several workers' deaths during a strike at the hands of the Police the previous day. It was a subdued affair, by the more honest accounts, that anywhere between 600-3,000 attended. Many had left by 10:30p.m., when the Police arrived in force and demanded that the crowd disperse. They were, with the speakers descending from the wagon, when a bomb was thrown killing 7 Policeman, 1 outright, 6 eventually. Later thought to be a provocateur posing as an anarchist, the culprit was never caught, nor perhaps even sought that hard. After this, gunfire scattered the square, leaving a further 60 Police officers wounded. Nobody knows how many demonstrators were either dead or wounded as they were too afraid to get official help and found it where they could. At the time rumours started that the demonstrators opened fire first. However, later anonymous reports pointed to Police fire only, who, in the resulting chaos were said to have "emptied" the contents of their revolvers on each other.

In the resulting clampdown many were arrested, particularly anarchists, with most of these associated with the radical German language workers' paper the *Arbeiter Zietung*. 8 were tried. Long-time activist Albert Parsons, whose wife was deemed "more dangerous than a thousand rioters", initially escaped arrest but walked into the courtroom on the day of the trial start to stand in solidarity with the others.

The trial was a blatant set up from start to finish, but public opinion was paranoid and strong. Even 7 years later, a pardon from Governor Altgeld, almost stating this, made him the most hated man in the U.S. for quite some time. The state and mainstream press brought the full weight of their might to bear on the men. Even before the rally the press shouted that Spies and Parsons should be made examples of, were there to be any trouble. Afterwards, they screamed, "Now it is blood" and continued to whip up frenzied copy for the remainder of the proceedings. It seems that organising is one thing, but combined with agitating (i.e. getting people to think critically or question authority) sends the establishment into turmoil. For this is where revolutions come from.

Judge Gary was openly hostile to the men and the jury rigged, most of whom also openly stated their prejudice against the defendants. The Police had long hated the men, who had not held back in their written and spoken exposure of Police corruption and brutality. Spies had been told by friends to watch his back as they had heard warnings of "getting even" after Spies had (unsuccessfully) tried to prosecute a Policeman for rape of a servant girl in custody. Neebe further accused them in his speech to the court and stood firm when Police Captain Schaak laughed at his words, saying that the Captain was an anarchist in the worst sense of the word. All through the case, the defendants were very articulate in their ideas on political anarchy and socialism, as opposed to capitalists, who they charged operated to the same violent anarchy that they were accused of. This, of course, was the real charge, that the men were picked out for being leaders and should be made examples of to "save our institutions, our society." The prosecutor even said at one point, "Anarchy is on trial".

On finding there was no evidence to prosecute for murder, as most of the men were not even present when the bomb was thrown, the judge swiftly changed the charge to one of conspiracy to incite the murders. Some had made bombs or had weapons, but the trial really centred on their written and spoken views on the sometimes legitimate use of violence. Eventually (surprise!), he found that their guilt to this equated to their guilt for murder and sentenced 1 to life in prison and 7 to death. Spies wryly noted that the principle of "a life for a life" was in action, relating to the 7 Police who lost their lives.

All the men spoke to the court nearing the end of the trial in October 1886 (the speeches in the records are well worth reading[2]). They are passionate, eloquent, and unyielding in their defence of themselves and their beliefs. They do not advocate violence at any cost, but they also do not rule it out either. They do not hold back their accusations levelled at the state and its agents and at capitalism generally. The phrase "speaking truth to power" was never so apt. By all accounts Samuel Fielden wowed the crowd with his oratory skill, ironically learnt as a Methodist preacher in Lancashire in the U.K. Albert Parsons spoke for a total of 8 hours over 2 days.

It is, however, August Spies' words that thrill me. In his speech, Spies is insistent and clever. He fiercely

> Revolutions are no more made than earthquakes and cyclones. Revolutions are the effect of certain causes and conditions.

2   http://www.chicagohistory.org/hadc/books/b01/B01TOC.htm

THE FIRE IS HERE

and fearlessly picks apart the arguments of his accusers. He uses natural phenomena to illustrate his point that anarchy and revolution are natural states. That a force can be brought to try to push us down but this can never stop us. We rise. We grow. No-one can stop the inevitable growth of the land, its people, and the forces that we contain. Change is the only constant and revolution is ever present in all beings' spirit and lungs.

He uses all the elements in his arguments:

Earth and air: "Revolutions are no more made than earthquakes and cyclones. Revolutions are the effect of certain causes and conditions... If anyone is to be blamed for the coming revolution it is the ruling class who steadily refused to make concessions as reforms became necessary; who maintain that they can call a halt to progress, and dictate a stand-still to the eternal forces, of which they themselves are but the whimsical creation."

Water: "You, in your blindness, think you can stop the tidal wave of civilization and human emancipation by placing a few policemen, a few Gatling guns, and some regiments of militia on the shore. You think you can frighten the rising waves back into the unfathomable depths, whence they have arisen, by erecting a few gallows in the perspective."

The fires of Beltane in a statement of perfect defiance: "If you think that by hanging us, you can stamp out the labor movement—the movement from which the downtrodden millions, the millions who toil and live in want and misery... if this is your opinion, then hang us! Here we will tread upon a spark, but there, and there, and behind you and in front of you, and everywhere, flames will blaze up. It is a subterranean fire. You cannot put it out. The ground is on fire upon which you stand."

Spies sets out a path but also a challenge to us all. This Beltane, where are you speaking truth to power despite the consequences? Where do you set your fires? How will you blaze up?

I have used Spies' words in the following poem about Beltane, rising up, and revolutions. It is dedicated to him and all the Haymarket martyrs, in memory of whom International May Day is now internationally observed (the first strikes for the 8-hour day were held on May 1st, 1886). I have also used a phrase from Dylan Thomas' poem, "The force that through the green fuse drives the flower" because, really, no other term will do...

"everything breathes
the revolutionary spirit"

for august spies

now is our time, we rise, we grow,
those voices strangled on mayday,
silent resolve most powerful
of bright green emancipation.
we force through, we a tidal wave,
come summer, come the early spring
that we may swell to our full height
to die, hunker over winter,
we the "green fuse" that refuses.

Nina George

Nina George is a social activist and writer living in Lancashire in North West England. She has worked on repairing the damage done by men who are abusive towards women for over 20 years. She agitates for revolution whenever she can.

The Sickness and the Medicine

Deconstructing Local Mythologies

Alley Valkyrie

The Willamette Valley stretches over 200 miles north-to-south along the Willamette River in Western Oregon. Cradled by mountain ranges to the east and west, the valley branches out northwards from the mountains outside of Eugene up through Salem and then past Portland, where the Willamette River meets the Columbia River at the Washington border. The valley is renowned for its rich and fertile soil, a result of volcanic glacial deposits from the Missoula Floods at the end of the last ice age, and the area is world-famous for its lush, old-growth forests as well as its agricultural output.

The Willamette Valley is also world-famous for its prevalence and severity of hay-fever allergies. The valley registers the highest grass pollen counts in the nation on a regular basis, and it was recently stated that Eugene in particular has the highest grass pollen counts in the world. The severity of the pollen varies seasonally as well as yearly, but it's especially high throughout May and June, and on the worst days many do not even leave their house due to breathing difficulties. Visitors to the area are often surprised to find themselves violently sneezing out of nowhere, especially if they don't normally suffer from hay-fever back home where they live. Local residents enjoy pointing out the fact that nobody is immune from the effects of the pollen. Many are often quick to share a well-known local myth in order to drive home the severity of allergy season in the Willamette Valley.

I initially heard the myth on my very first visit to the Pacific Northwest, long before I ever called the Willamette Valley home. I was sitting at a counter in a restaurant just outside of Eugene, my backpack next to me. I started to sneeze profusely, and the man sitting next to me glanced over at me in my sinus-based misery. "You know, 'Willamette' is an Indian word meaning 'valley of sickness' or something close to that," he said to me. "The allergies were so bad here that when white folks first came over the [Oregon] Trail, the Indians warned 'em not to settle here. They thought that we were crazy for doing so."

The story immediately sounded suspect to me. At the time, I knew nothing of the history of the Willamette Valley, but I did know that far too often, "history" that references Native people is anything but truthful or accurate. As a product of American public schools, I was taught for years on end that Columbus "discovered" America and that the Pilgrims and Indians gathered for a happy Thanksgiving feast. Growing up in the New York City area, I was taught as accepted "fact" that Peter Minuit "purchased" Manhattan from a local tribe for $24. Stories such as these are accepted as "history" to many, and yet they are well-known to be heavily sanitized and mythologized in order to de-emphasize the oppression and colonialism that are central to their true history. I had a hunch at that moment in the restaurant that the "valley of sickness" tale I had just been told was nothing more than sanitized mythology in the same vein as Columbus or Minuit, and yet it was obvious by his telling of the tale that the man next to me believed it as factual truth and fully expected me to believe it as well.

A few years later, after I moved to Eugene, I immediately started to hear variations of the "valley of sickness" tale on a regular basis, told by people from all walks of life. There were many slight variations of the myth, as expected with any folklore. Often I heard it told as the valley of "death" as opposed to "sickness". Once in a while, someone would say that "the Indians nicknamed this the valley of sickness", as opposed to claiming that the word "Willamette" itself literally translates as such. In some versions, the Indians left and/or didn't want to live here because of the pollen, and other times they just warned white settlers not to settle here. The basic story is always the same, however. And as opposed to commonly-held beliefs around Columbus, I never heard anyone refute nor even question the "valley of sickness" tale.

After hearing several versions of the tale within the first few months of my living here, it occurred to me that not only was this tale most likely false, but that I was quite disconnected from the history of this valley that I chose as home. Prior to moving to Oregon, I had lived my entire life within a 100-mile radius of New York City, and I was quite well-versed in the history of the New York area, from the landing of the Mayflower through the present. That knowledge, especially as it relates to the land itself, became central to my spiritual exploration and practice when I lived on the East Coast. Researching and examining the history of place in relation to the activities, energies and present tendencies within that place was a source of constant fascination for me, and became essential to my practice in terms of navigating a dense urban landscape from an energetic perspective.

Here in Oregon, however, while I had a decent understanding of the local culture, I knew nothing of the actual history of either Eugene in itself or the Willamette Valley as a whole. I felt a need to connect to both the timeline-based history of this valley as well as to the land itself, and I decided to start educating myself in local history using the "valley of sickness" tale as a starting point.

I broke down the tale in order to identify the basic alleged facts within the story. If any or all parts of the tale have any truth to them, then any or all of the individual facts within the story need to carry some truth:

that high pollen counts were an issue
in the 1850s;

that the native people who inhabited the land prior
to white settlement were adversely affected by the
pollen;

that "willamette" is a native word that translates to
"valley of sickness";

and/or that "willamette" does not specifically translate as such but the native inhabitants also gave the valley another nickname that translated to "valley of sickness";

and/or that the native inhabitants discouraged white
settlers from settling in the area due
to the pollen;

that the native inhabitants left because of all the pollen and related sickness;

and/or the native people never lived here in
large numbers in the first place because of
all the pollen.

THE FIRE IS HERE

With this outline as a guide, I immersed myself in the history of the Willamette Valley and its present conditions. And indeed, I learned quickly that the "valley of sickness" tale was a multi-layered falsehood served to deny and mask the injustices done to the native inhabitants of this area. The truth itself did not surprise me as much as how easy the truth was to find for anyone who cared to look for it. A few books combined with a few conversations gave me all the answers I needed.

Prior to white settlement, the Willamette Valley was originally inhabited by the Kalapuya, a semi-nomadic tribe who migrated within the valley for centuries before Europeans ever set foot in Oregon. Lewis and Clark first passed through the Willamette Valley in 1806, and the fur trappers and missionaries came through the area soon thereafter, bringing with them smallpox, measles, and other diseases to which the Kalapuya had no immunity. These diseases ravaged the Kalapuya population through the mid-1800s, with some sources estimating that over 90% of the Kalapuya had died by the time that the first wave of white settlers came through the Willamette Valley from the Oregon Trail in the early 1850s.

The remaining Kalapuya referred to the Willamette Valley as the "valley of sickness" after the settlers came, but it was due to smallpox, not hay-fever. Some of the remaining Kalapuya may have migrated elsewhere on account of the widespread sickness, but the rest were removed to a reservation in 1855. The word "Willamette" itself derives from a Chinook word, and there is no definitive record as to its precise meaning. Most historians and scholars agree that it most likely referred to the water and/or specifically the river, and that the word pre-dates the smallpox epidemic and has nothing to do with sickness or pollen.

The native terrain of the Willamette Valley was mostly composed of prairie-savannahs and wetlands, with a mix of surrounding coniferous forests. The Kalapuya were hunter-gatherers, not farmers, and did not plant or cultivate crops. Various histories of the Kalapuya make no mention of excessive pollen or hay-fever, and there is nothing specific that stands out in the botanical and/or ecological composition of the Willamette Valley prior to white settlement that would give cause for the excessive pollen counts, especially such excessive pollen from any one plant source such as grass.

In contrast, the present-day Willamette Valley is a major agricultural center, and commercial non-native grass seed is by far the most prevalent crop. Grass seed production in the Willamette Valley was introduced in the 1920's, and currently the valley produces nearly two-thirds of the nation's grass seed. Production in acreage recently peaked at nearly 500,000 acres, and currently nearly 1,500 farms are devoted to grass seed, many of which are owned by national and multinational seed companies. The highest grass pollen counts in the world and the subsequent hay-fever allergies are essentially a direct result of a $250 million-dollar industry that is significantly shielded from blame by the widespread proliferation of the "valley of sickness" tale. But due to the commonly-held belief that residents of the Willamette Valley have been sneezing nonstop since the 1850s, a typical sneezer in Eugene is often completely unaware of the fact that the elevated pollen levels that cause

> The truth itself did not surprise me as much as how easy the truth was to find for anyone who cared to look for it.

A BEAUTIFUL RESISTANCE

such severe allergies are mainly caused by commercial grass seed production as opposed to the local trees and plants in the immediate area.

As an outsider in this community, it was initially hard for me to understand why the myth was so prevalent and widespread despite easily accessible information that disproves the story entirely. It was also hard for me to understand the mindsets of several people I encountered who were very aware that at least one or more core factual elements of the tale were untrue. When I asked them if they ever corrected people on the facts, most of them admitted that they did not. "The story is appealing," one woman told me, defending her silence. "I don't want to be the bearer of bad vibes." I disagreed strongly with her stance, but over time I understood her point more than I wished to admit. In a town full of back-to-the-land hippies and leftist intellectuals who are often all-too caught up in a culture of positive affirmations and passive-aggressive niceties, nobody wants to be the one bringing up genocide in the middle of a barbecue.

But over the years, when I look deep into the eyes of the myth itself time and time again, as well as into the eyes of the people who tell it, I have come to understand its appeal within the context of the local culture, especially given the fact that most of those who tell it are white, middle-class folks who are either the descendants of pioneers or transplants from other parts of the country. The myth serves as an easy explanation for the pollen issues, and it connects modern inhabitants of the Willamette Valley with the native people who lived here before them. There's a sense of comfort inherent in the idea that even indigenous tribes hundreds of years ago suffered from hay-fever as people do today. Many also feel that the myth demonstrates the wisdom of the native inhabitants, and they feel that by telling the tale they are honoring that wisdom. "The Native Americans were right," a friend said to me recently, in the midst of a hay-fever spell during one of the highest pollen measurements on record. "They warned us not to settle here, and man were they right."

> The highest grass pollen counts in the world and the subsequent hay-fever allergies are essentially a direct result of a $250 million-dollar industry.

And yet, the myth is oppressive and damaging on many levels. The myth falsely explains away the modern suffering of those who benefited from colonialism at the expense of the truth behind the suffering of those who were oppressed by the colonizers. Not only does the "valley of sickness" tale dishonor the legacy and memory of the Kalapuya by whitewashing the truth of their history and suffering, but the myth also dishonors the spirits and ancestors of this valley that lived and experienced that truth. The fact that the myth also protects multinational agribusinesses whose profit-driven actions wreak havoc on the health of the people in addition to disrupting the native ecosystem is simply the icing on the cake, especially in an area where local values tend to be left-leaning and anti-corporate in principle.

Deconstructing this myth taught me many lessons, and gave me many insights into the local history and culture that have been invaluable to me ever since. More importantly, my questions regarding the myth not only revealed to me my own disconnect with the history of the land, but the fact that most who live here are ignorant of their own history, both the history of

THE FIRE IS HERE

their ancestors as well as the history of this valley itself. My disconnect was due to being an outsider, and to some extent it is the outsider's perspective that inspired me to develop the relationships and understandings that I have with the land and the culture of the Willamette Valley. Researching the myth also brought me in contact for the first time with the energies and spirits of this land, a relationship which has greatly deepened over time and has become essential to my work as a community activist and amateur historian.

It's currently allergy season, and I've heard the "valley of sickness" tale twice this week alone. And while I can't prevent its telling, nor can I necessarily deflate its ubiquity, I can strongly dent its armor in subtle ways. But rather than lecturing people on genocide, oppression, and whitewashed history, I've found that the most effective method of drowning out such sanitized mythology is to simply tell a new story, one based in truth and fact.

And so I have become the awkward guest at the dinner party, so to speak, but I keep it short, sweet, and easy to digest. Whenever I hear the myth mentioned in my presence, my response has become almost automated. "That story is bullshit. The Kalapuya were sick with smallpox, not hay-fever, and pollen wasn't an issue in the valley until agribusiness moved in. If you don't like the hay-fever, blame the grass seed companies, but retelling that story only serves to disrespect the original inhabitants of the valley."

Once in a while, in the midst of debunking the myth, I often sense something in the wind. I take it as a reminder that the land is always listening.

Alley Valkyrie

Alley Valkyrie is a writer, artist, and spirit-worker currently living in the part of occupied Chinook territory that white settlers renamed 'Portland, Oregon'. She has been interacting with a various collection of gods and radicals for over fifteen years. When she's not plotting in various ways to take down Capitalism, Alley works with homeless folks, communes with crows and bees, and writes for The Wild Hunt.

The Year of the Black Lake

Lauren Lockhart

Rusted threads of prophecy run up her arm,
sepsis aligning with the threshold,

coming out of the corner with death frosted on the
buffered panes of our sleep—

we are healed by what can end us.
There is no place safe from dreaming.

There sprouts the tender beginnings of a blade from
some heaving obstruction between still blood and running,

a sore pit in the eyes of our understanding.
Brackish and inky, a lake in the night—

so much like the knife where there is nothing living
and it is churning with life.

Bind your boldness, then, to intent and the green branches
which point away from the waiting water.

Coma will lull the drowning further,
black silt tilting your head back it

fills your nose and throat with finality, dim water
snatches inflammation and tightness away from you and slips under.

It takes courage to close your eyes.

Lauren Lockhart

Lauren is a queer-witch poet, a practicing Druid and student of Sethian Gnosticism. She dabbles in divination, trance-mediumship and works closely with plants. Based in the Pacific Northwest, Lauren is studying Community Acupuncture to ensure that trauma-informed, affordable health care continues to expand its reach and serve marginalized populations.

The Dangers Facing Seneca Lake

Joe DiCicco

There is an issue of dire importance facing the upstate region of New York, an issue that has the potential to negatively impact over 100,000 people and countless animal and plant wildlife. Up here, a good four to five hours northwest of the city, you have the region of the state known as the Finger Lakes. Beautiful lake country to some, fly-over-land to others. The economy is crumbling, the culture is lacking, at best. Like many places around the country and indeed the world, good-paying, full-time jobs are few and far between. However, there is an established winery industry here, and a growing beer brewing industry. You might say it's the type of place that's great for business owners in these industries, as well as tourists, but it might be less than ideal for anyone else. Sure, there may be plenty of jobs in the summertime, but the majority of these are often very part-time, and minimum wage to boot. Anyone driving from town to town searching for someone to give them a solid full-time job with benefits might find themselves empty-handed in a frigid land peppered with small towns, ancient churches, long-abandoned storefronts and decrepit mills and factories that at one point may have offered jobs one could raise a family with. There is also very likely a Walmart just on the edge of any of these towns and hamlets.

Maybe I'm being too harsh. Maybe it's not that bad. It all depends on where you fit in the region known as the Finger Lakes. The natural landscape is quite beautiful, with forests, glens, plenty of hiking and scenic trails, not to mention four seasons. Plenty of natural resources. Unfortunately, it is these resources that so often attract the gluttonous appetite of runaway capitalism.

The region gets its name from the eleven beautiful and ancient freshwater lakes so many here take for granted. These lakes are no less than priceless. The largest, and arguably the most beautiful is the lake known as Seneca. The Haudenosaunee (Iroquois) people native to the area believed that God lay his hand onto the land to create these lakes. Some would say Seneca Lake is the middle finger. This is where the 100,000 people come into play.

At thirty-eight miles long and two miles wide, Seneca is over six hundred feet deep. The majority of the region's booming wine industry is peppered all along this lake, with more wineries than all but the most raging of alcoholics can count.

But this precious lake is quite literally under attack. A Texas-based company, Crestwood Midstream[3], has set its sights on storing 88 million gallons of liquid propane and butane a mere one mile from the shoreline in natural, unlined salt caverns. The exact type of caverns which are known to be prone to collapse. The vast majority of the local community is steadfastly against this project, including every single town and village that gets its water from the lake. Except one.

3   http://www.crestwoodlp.com/home/default.aspx

A BEAUTIFUL RESISTANCE

The one little village that supports this ridiculous project is the one that would see the payout in the terms of a community benefits agreement and a business on the tax rolls. None of the others matter, it would seem, despite all of them relying on this lake for the continuance of life.

Two grassroots-level groups have sprung up in opposition to this project; Gas Free Seneca[4] and We Are Seneca Lake[5]. These two groups have organized numerous blockades at the gates of the proposed storage facility on the lake, creating human walls and holding signs in defense of our lake, as well as our Mother Earth, in general. These blockades have stopped countless trucks from entering the facility, and thus far, there has been not one incidence of violence, destructive behavior or resisting arrest. Any resisting charge would come from the fact that as of October 2014, nearly 500 different protesters have been arrested at these gates. The local sheriffs and state police can't seem to arrest them fast enough. The protesters, mostly older adults, are school teachers, medical professionals, and even religious clergy. Many of them are in their 60s and some in their 70s. One man, a Navy veteran, was 86 years old standing in front of the gates to his, and our, lake. Like many of the protesters, he was slapped with a $350 fine, which he refused to pay, instead opting to do two weeks in county jail. I can't imagine doing a two-week stint behind bars at 31, and this gentleman did it at 86. And he wasn't done. The very day he got out, he returned immediately to those gates to rejoin the blockade. In fact, my former college professor from when I studied environmental conservation at Finger Lakes Community College has been heavily involved in the resistance to this potentially hazardous project, and he is in his 70s.

What we're seeing here is the desperate, mad-grab of an industry that I, and many others, hope is on its death bed. We have the technology to pursue cleaner, healthier and more sustainable energy resources. The problem is we have a long-standing industry utterly vested in seeing that it does not happen.

Crestwood Midstream has the gall to claim any opponents to the project who do not live on the very shores of the lake are *outside agitators*. Now this has me squinting and wondering. The company from halfway across the country that wants to come to New York and risk potentially catastrophic tragedy on our lake is not the *outside agitator*, but I, who live a mere 10 to 15 miles from the lakeshore and drink its waters every day, am? This is a perfect example of the dangerous and potentially deadly logic so often used by self-serving corporate interests in the name of the almighty bottom line.

Another real knee-slapper is the comical amount of jobs the entire project aims to create. Are you ready? 10 to 15 jobs. In all. Total. An out-of-state fossil fuel storage company wants to put the drinking water of 100,000 human beings and countless animal and plant life at risk to create 10 to 15 jobs.

I want to laugh, I really do. I want to shake my head and slap my knee and enjoy the zany comedy movie I'm watching. Except it's not a movie, and it sure as hell is no comedy. It's really happening. And it's happening at full-force, break-neck speed. The logic is flawed at best, totally non-sensical at worst. And it is only the tip of an incredibly sinister iceberg: the privatization by corporate interests of freshwater sources. One could dig deeper into the issue and find entire lakes and rivers out west that are being bought for water distributors. But that is another issue and I will not get into it here.

Fresh, clean drinking water is beyond crucial. It is a necessity - the building block of life as we know it. I cannot overstate how important it is. But I fear it has simply been taken for granted for too long. It's always been here, so most just assume it always will be. But my lake, Seneca Lake, has been growing more and more salinated as the years and decades go by, mostly from industry, and winery runoff. It has already been found

4 http://gasfreeseneca.com/
5 http://www.wearesenecalake.com/

in an independent study done by Seneca Lake Pure Waters Association[6] to be too salty for young children and anyone on a low-sodium diet. This lake simply cannot take any more stress. And to put more stress on her for the sake of 10 to 15 jobs is at best, plainly offensive, and at worst, an act of aggression on the 100,000 residents and beautiful ecosystem of the Finger Lakes region.

[6] http://senecalake.org/

Joe DiCicco

Joe DiCicco is a 31-year-old writer from New York. He mostly writes fiction, but has recently begun tackling issues of importance, such as environmental concerns. He has a degree in Natural Resources Conservation.

Song of the swollen cells

Nimue Brown

These bones are rock made
From my birth land, water carried.
This skin is plant, creature
A lifetime of chewing one form
Into another.

Every tree has beauty,
But not I.
Somehow instead, a bloating,
Like the drowned, the dead.
Puffball expanding towards explosion.

In otters, the river's poison met,
Tributaries of death ran to pool
In fat cells and reproductive organs.
A brush with extinction.

I drank my bones from these
Same otter killing rivers.
I breathed the motorway, I ate
Pesticides and worse.
Fat cell storage holds this
And more, and how much?

Generations of ancestral shame
Ride my hips like a girdle.
Anger taken in, injustice
Part of my flesh.

My body a rainforest made ready
For the palm oil plantation.
My body landscape to be fracked

In commercial exploitation.
My body the sacred land.

How can I be Pagan and not
Raise the tainted cup to my lips?
How can I not drink of the river?
What bones are these
Made from a quest for hydrocarbons.
What bones are these
Unable to support the weight
Of a people bloated from eating
The bodies we killed with poison.

Oh, for the quiet of rocks
The otter-embracing river
And cells unsaturated
With other people's madness.

Nimue Brown

Nimue Brown writes Pagan titles for Moon Books, and fiction in various forms. She blogs regularly at www.druidlife.com. Trained by OBOD, she has a somewhat improvised, feral approach to Druidry, preferring rituals that start 'hello sky, hello hill,' to more formal approaches. Her current obsession is with stories in the landscape.

Only Connect

Yvonne Aburrow

There is a view of life in which events are not perceived as connected, people are seen as separate entities, mere expendable units to be crushed under the wheels of the great machine known as 'progress'. It was this view that prevailed during the Irish Potato Famine in the nineteenth century, when full grain ships were allowed to leave Irish ports because 'market forces' meant that their contents could be sold elsewhere rather than being used to feed the starving farm workers.

In his great novel, *Howard's End*, E. M. Forster presented an extended critique of this view. Two middle class sisters befriend a young working class man, who ends up dying. The husband of one of the sisters cannot see that he is in any way responsible for the young man's death, despite the fact that it is intimately bound up with all the other events of the novel. The novel is an extended illustration of its epigraph, "Only connect". If I had to sum up my philosophy in two words, it would be those two words.

...she might yet be able to help him to the building of the rainbow bridge that should connect the prose in us with the passion. Without it we are meaningless fragments, half monks, half beasts, unconnected arches that have never joined into a man. With it love is born, and alights on the highest curve, glowing against the grey, sober against the fire. Happy the man who sees from either aspect the glory of these outspread wings. The roads of his soul lie clear, and he and his friends shall find easy-going.... It did not seem so difficult. She need trouble him with no gift of her own. She would only point out the salvation that was latent in his own soul, and in the soul of every man. Only connect! That was the whole of her sermon. Only connect the prose and the passion, and both will be exalted, and human love will be seen at its height. Live in fragments no longer. Only connect and the beast and the monk, robbed of the isolation that is life to either, will die.

E. M. Forster, Howard's End, chapter XXII

But the novel is not simply about *making* the connection between the inner and the outer, the beast and the angel in us, but also *seeing* the connections between different aspects of life, and different circum-

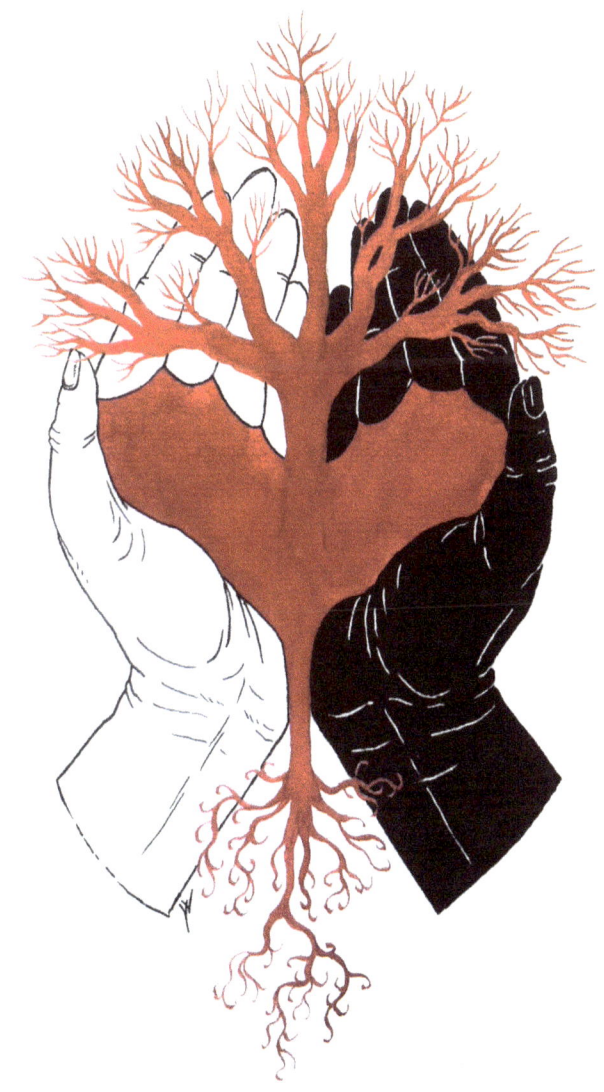

THE FIRE IS HERE

stances. The young working class man is crushed by the middle class man's inability to connect, to see the lights and shadows. He is crushed by the whole social system in which the characters are trapped. E. M. Forster, himself a socialist and a friend of the great radical pioneer of the late nineteenth century, Edward Carpenter (a gay Pagan socialist vegetarian anarchist), was trying – ever so gently – to point out that the whole capitalist and hierarchical system was built to destroy life, love, and pleasure.

Once we start to see the connections between one circumstance and another, they cannot be unseen. If you look at the whole system of property, capital, profit, race, class, and kyriarchal oppression, and start to trace it back to its roots, you can see that the parts of the system are not independent of each other, but developed together. This makes the system of oppression hard to unravel if you only try to tackle it piecemeal, and don't see the connections between the different parts.

If you look at the alternative ways of living that people have tried to create over the last few centuries, you can see that they are also a set of interconnected ideas and practices. Different co-operative, p/Pagan, spiritual, Dissenting, anarchist, socialist, and communitarian groups evolved out of each other, shared ideas, and built similar alternative structures. In trying to create a vision of an alternative society, we don't have to reinvent the wheel, as the effort to create something different has been building momentum for a while.

The interconnected kyriarchy

The kyriarchy – the hierarchical view of human relations, built on power over others, and regarding those others as lesser beings, perhaps not even human, has been with us for more than two millennia. In *Truth or Dare*, Starhawk[7] put forward the idea that it came about because of farming. As hunter-gatherers settled down and started to farm the land, they started to regard the land as belonging to them. The population got larger. They also needed to irrigate the land, and this led to over-salination. As more and more fields became unworkable, land became scarce, and this gave rise to war. War meant that warriors, who were usually male, were now the most valued members of society. In order to kill another human being, warriors needed to see them as other, as less than human. And so the whole system of hierarchy, war, kings, and power-over came about. The new system also meant that because men were the most valued members of society, inheritance passed through the male line, which meant that women's sexuality had to be controlled. This kyriarchal view of existence fed into the Roman Empire, which co-opted Christianity around the time of the Council of Nicaea (325 CE).

By 500 CE, the lack of connection between the spiritual and the physical had reached such a pitch that there was a highly toxic and misogynist view of all things fleshly, especially women. Every time a small group of people tried to build a radical communitarian way of life, whether on political or religious grounds, or both, they were crushed, but another group rose from the ruins and carried on.

In England, after the Norman invasion, the land rights of the local population were taken away. It has taken centuries of struggle, and we still have not entirely recovered them. There were the appropriation of Saxon lands, especially forest, by the new Norman overlords; the Acts of Enclosure, which took away common land, so memorably bemoaned by the poet John Clare; the regulation of rights to forage, and the imposition of heavy fines and penalties for any infringement. In Scotland, the Highland Clearances involved much the same kind of theft of lands and livelihoods of ordinary people. The excellent travelling show and website *Three Acres and a Cow*, performed by Robin Grey (who recently shot to fame as the busker who suggested that David Cameron should 'fuck off back to Eton'[8]) and Rachel Rose Reid, documents the history

---

7 Starhawk (1988), *Truth or Dare: Encounters with Power, Authority and Mystery*. (San Francisco, HarperSanFrancisco). http://starhawk.org/writing/books/truthordare/

8 A Quick Chat With The Busker Who Sang "F*ck Off Back To Eton" At David Cameron - Buzzfeed http://www.buzzfeed.com/

of resistance to the theft of land by the ruling classes, from the Norman Conquest, via the Peasants' Revolt, to the Enclosures and the Highland Clearances, and links these with today's issues of housing shortages, fracking, and food.

In America, lands and livelihood, labour and the fruits of labour, were stolen from indigenous people, and from enslaved people. Just for a moment it looked as if Thomas Morton would set up an alternative community at Merry Mount, but it too was crushed.

All of these thefts and appropriations stem from the view that some people are inherently worth more than others, by 'virtue' of their ability to crush dissent, subdue others, and get more money and power. They stem from the idea that land can be property, and is not held in common for the benefit of all. This hierarchical and commodified view of the worth of people and land (instead of viewing them as intrinsically sacred) gave rise to war, enslavement, rape, and torture. All of these horrors are made possible by viewing the victim as worth less than the perpetrator; othering them and devaluing them.

This hierarchical and commodified view of value was made much worse by capitalism, which disconnected the workers from the work of their hands, and alienated them, by introducing mass production. By valuing the profits due to the investors and shareholders over giving a living wage to the workers, workers were stripped of their humanity and became mere cogs in the machine.

chrisstokelwalker/thefuckoffbacktoetonbuskerisonatraint17b68

The Whig interpretation of history would have you believe that the ruling classes came to their senses by themselves and distributed resources more evenly. However, even just looking at the last decade in the UK, we can see that this is not true, because the ruling classes and the rich have grabbed more money and power – in the form of the privatisation of education, prisons, and the health service, payouts to bankers, tax evasion, and vastly inflated salaries (one particular University Vice-Chancellor gets paid more than the Prime Minister, for example). All of this has led to a massive widening of the gap between rich and poor.

The web of life

Fortunately there has always been resistance to the hierarchical and commodified view of humans and the natural world. There was the Peasants' Revolt, protest marches against Enclosures, the Diggers and Levellers, who tried to found a more equal and just society. There were the Reform Riots against mass starvation in the 1830s; the rally in London in protest against the deportation of the Tolpuddle Martyrs; the Chartist uprising. There was the mass trespass on Kinder Scout in 1933, where the factory workers of Manchester surged onto the surrounding moors, which had previously been reserved for the landowners who used them for shooting wildlife. There were rent strikes against extortionate rents; there was the co-operative movement which aimed to build an alternative economy. There was the struggle for liberation from slavery, and the women's rights movement. The struggle for women's rights arose out of the successful organising of women who campaigned against slavery. We can learn something from both the successes and failures of each of these movements: the horrific oppression they struggled against; the seeming insurmountability of the obstacles, and their eventual victory, however partial.

The Unitarian movement arose out of a radical religious group – the late 15th century humanists of North Italy, who fled first to Poland, and then to Transylvania. While they were in Poland, they had their own printing press and sent radical pamphlets to England, which fuelled a fresh wave of radical dissent. Eventually the Unitarians gave rise to Transcendentalism, which included such luminaries as Ralph Waldo Emerson, Theodore Parker, Nathaniel Hawthorne, and Walt Whitman, who corresponded with Edward Carpenter. Transcendentalism, according to Chas Clifton[9], was one of the strands that led into the Pagan revival. Many Unitarians and Transcendentalists were socialists, campaigners for the abolition of slavery, and at the forefront of women's rights. Two Unitarians, James Reeb and Viola Liuzzo, died after being attacked by racist thugs at Selma. In 2008, two Unitarian Universalists, Linda Kraeger and Greg McKendry, were killed in an attack on Tennessee Valley UU, a church that actively supports LGBT rights.

In England, the Labour movement was born out of many strands of resistance, including Chartists, trade unions, the co-operative movement, socialists, feminists, and anarchists. The Arts and Crafts movement was founded by socialists, who sought to restore dignity and beauty to craftsmanship, and reforge the connection between the maker and the made, which had been so brutally severed by the alienation caused by mass production, where a made thing was no longer the work of one person, but the anonymous and uniform production of several workers.

One of the key figures in the early Labour movement was Edward Carpenter, who had links with both anarchists and socialists, and who wrote movingly on the restoration of the connection between people and Nature. He could be regarded as one of the founders of the Pagan revival, as he wrote extensively on the joys of Paganism, and made the connection between the Pagan revelry of May Day and the celebration of workers' rights. Sadly, he is largely forgotten today by both Pagans and socialists, perhaps because he was gay and was sidelined during the excessively homophobic period of the 1950s, but his ideas are enjoying a revival amongst gay men, and have never been forgotten in his adopted city of Sheffield.

A study of all the different radical movements of the last 400 years would reveal a fascinating web of connections between the people and ideas involved in them.

A study of all the different radical movements of the last 400 years would reveal a fascinating web of connections between the people and ideas involved in them.

Recently, the excellent film *Pride* revealed the connection between the miners' strike in the mid-1980s and LGBT rights in the UK. Lesbians and gay men formed a support group to raise funds for the miners during the darkest days of the strike, and in return, the unions who represent the miners voted *en bloc* for Labour policies supporting LGBT rights (such as the repeal of section 28, the lower-

9   Chas S. Clifton (2006), *Her Hidden Children: The Rise of Wicca and Paganism in America (Pagan Studies Series)*, Altamira Press

A BEAUTIFUL RESISTANCE

ing of the age of consent for same-sex partners to the same age as for opposite-sex partners, and the introduction of same-sex marriage).

The ability to connect with someone else's struggle, even in the midst of your own struggle, can give rise to unexpected results. After the abolition of slavery, many Black abolitionists supported the cause of women's rights, just as women had campaigned for the abolition of slavery. The solidarity of trade unionists around the world has led to many victories for freedom and democracy and human rights. The ability to connect your own experience of oppression with someone else's experience of oppression is the key to radical transformation.

The power of the internet to enable rapid communication between movements resisting hegemonic oppression and capitalist exploitation around the world has been a key lever in helping them to build connections. Irish activists resisting Shell in Ireland have linked up with Nigerian activists doing the same in the Niger delta. Recently I have attended two demonstrations about the UK's racist immigration policy, both of which were mobilised via the internet. Groups resisting capitalism and racism can make and maintain connections, both over the internet, and at May Day rallies and other events. I was pleased to see that the trades union banner at the May Day Rally in Oxford, UK, expressed solidarity with Baltimore and the Black Lives Matter campaign.

At the moment, with the re-election of a Conservative government in the UK, the right-wing governments in Australia and Canada, and the seemingly relentless systemic racism in the US, it seems as if there is no hope of change. However, the Province of Alberta has just elected a left-wing government for the first time in 40 years, and the people of Greece have sent a resounding anti-austerity message by voting in a left-wing government. The tide is turning. People are beginning to see that there must be another way to live than greed, consumption, and exploitation.

People are beginning to make the connection between the sacredness of the Earth, the waters, the animals, the birds, and the people.

People are beginning to reconnect with the gods and spirits of the land, recognising that returning to right relationship with the land, making deep connections with place and community, making loving connections with others, is the key to harmony and indeed survival, both physical and spiritual.

By recognising the sacredness of the land, the idea that no-one can own it, and that it must be held in common for the benefit of all beings, we radically reaffirm our connection to nature.

By recognising the sacredness of the body and of pleasure, we reconnect to our very instincts, and the gods-given pleasures of the flesh.

By connecting our present predicament with the threads of oppression and resistance woven for us by our ancestors, we can begin to unravel destructive ways of being, and begin to weave new possibilities, drawing on the bright threads of dissent and revolutionary ways of being from the past.

By connecting our own hopes and dreams with those of others around the world who are reaching for new ways of being, we can learn from each other and strengthen our own visions, and correct our cultural biases by seeing with multiple perspectives from different cultures.

By connecting with the struggles of others, we reaffirm our humanity.

Yvonne Aburrow

Yvonne Aburrow is genderqueer, bisexual, a polytheist Wiccan, and an anarchist socialist green leftie feminist. Her most recent book is All Acts of Love and Pleasure: Inclusive Wicca. *She has also written four books on mythology, and two anthologies of poetry. She co-edited* Pagan Consent Culture *with Christine Hoff-Kraemer.*

THE FIRE IS HERE

WE ARE LIVING ON TURTLE ISLAND

– Isn't it Time We Started Acting that Way?

Pegi Eyers

It continues to astound me that the dialogue about apocalypse readiness, the old paradigm dying and the new world being built here in the Americas, continues to ignore the values and earth-embedded lifeways as modelled to us by the First Nations, the original inhabitants of these lands. As children of the western paradigm and the colonizer class who brought civilization to these shores, are we so sure of our status here on Turtle Island that our Pagan, anti-civ or rewilding thought and action systems don't need to reference what came before? Why are First Nations so invisible, and rarely mentioned in our work to become reconnected to nature spiritualities? Are we that comfortable that our own Gods and Goddesses and ancestral traditions made the transition from Europe safely, or as interloper-aliens, are other claims to the land still in play? These are not idle questions to be sure.

Celebrating the death throes of capitalism and installing a blend of old and new holistic values into our lives is the great work, and mutual decolonization also offers us the opportunity to heal our fractured relationship with First Nations. But first, we need to unpack all the mistakes our cultural group has been making. Historically speaking and well into contemporary times, here on Turtle Island white people have related to indigenous people in predictable ways. Starting with the research methods of anthropology and ethnography, followed by the stereotypes and romanticization that develop from a love/hate dynamic, to questionable trends in our spiritual life that actually harm while professing to admire, we continue with the assumption that a First Nations acquaintance or wisdom keeper represents the opinions of all First Nations people (which is known as "tokenizing"). And indigenous people were not originally consulted on the matter, but it has become cohesively clear over the years that the practice of cultural appropriation is an extension of racism, white privilege and the hierarchy of the oppressor/oppressed relationship in the Americas. As the descendants of the first Settlers (or those more recently emigrated to the Americas) guess which side of that dynamic Pagans, Druids, Polytheists and Animists are on?

In recent times drawing close to First Nations has become a highly competitive game, insular and cliquey, with those using their white privilege to get to as many exotic indigenous locations as possible, and having accumulated a wealth of First Nations connections and spiritual teachings, to play the "holier than thou" hand with their own white cohort. These folks are accomplished with the "My Elder is better than your Elder" exchange, have "transcended" any kind of conversation on cultural appropriation, are more spiritual than other white seekers (certainly more "indigenous!") and are better placed to set themselves up as gurus for the rest of us. Also, the quest for adoring white folks to be "adopted in" by indulging in "Elder Essentialism" gives them a great outlet for the expression of their never-ending spiritual feelings and UPG (unverified personal gnosis), allows them to wear rustic or patterned indigenous garb, and enables their "higher calling" as channelers, "shamans," healers and drum makers. Unfortunately, all these approaches are more about the white person than the actual lives and diverse realities of genuine contemporary First Nations individuals and communities, who continue to suffer the fallout from cultural genocide.

After examining the full range of these inventive "Settler Sidesteps" we finally arrive at the most ethical and best engagement, which are relationships grounded in *Allyship Theory* and social justice solidarity. Regardless of the extent to which First Nations folks have been assimilated and exhibit the behaviors we are comfortable with in our own white culture(s), by far the vast majority of indigenous leaders and communities are occupied with rejuvenating their own specific indigenous knowledge and traditions, and continue to fight for land, nationhood, sovereignty, their constitutionally-protected and internationally-recognized treaty rights, and the basic human rights that the rest of us take for granted. When we become allies to First Nations and assist them in their anti-racism and anti-oppression efforts, we advance the cross-cultural learning that is integral to social justice struggles, and create radical change in ourselves, the community and the world.

Allyship Theory is an excellent framework that allows us to have accountable, ethical ways of working with marginalized groups. In this dynamic, indigenous people provide the leadership and allies take action in support of the direction that has been determined. We are not heroes or heroines riding in on a white horse to save everybody (!), we are assisting a group of people who already have a plan in place. It takes much humility to set aside our privilege and bias, to listen to First Nations, and place their needs at the center. This is what an Ally does, and this reversal of the habitual power relationship is essential to eliminating systemic racism. It is only by placing ourselves behind the most oppressed and helping them move forward, will true progress be made.

The first step to becoming an Ally is to learn the history of your region and the indigenous peoples who have lived there, and who live there now, so that they are not invisible to you. What are their current struggles? What are they thinking? What monumental work are they already doing in cultural revival, land ethics, intellectual discourse, human rights activism and decolonization? What are their successes and what are their ongoing challenges? Becoming familiar with the history and current issues of the indigenous community closest to you is key to the Ally process, as is extending the

> When we become allies to First Nations and assist them in their anti-racism and anti-oppression efforts, we advance the cross-cultural learning that is integral to social justice struggles, and create radical change in ourselves, the community and the world.

THE FIRE IS HERE

proper respect to the original inhabitants of Turtle Island.

The main challenge for allies to address in self and others is the denial of colonial violence, and the endemic lack of awareness regarding white privilege and the kyriarchy of intersectional oppressions. Social activism starts with self-education, *Rejecting Empire*, mobilizing (which is showing up for rallies, protests and actions), followed by long-term and strategic organizing in the community that can lead to successful coalitions. Speaking up and educating other white people about racism, white privilege, historical truth and the third world conditions that exist on Turtle Island is our role. Many First Nations live in disgraceful ghetto-like (de facto apartheid) conditions because of racism perpetuated by white people, and it is white people who need to reverse this hegemony. Rejecting the dominant white-led view of history, we need to consider racism, white privilege and history from the point of view of the oppressed.[10] And long-term Allyship requires that our solidarity relationships are based on the principles of decolonization, and that we are committed to the well-being and sovereignty of the indigenous community as a whole.

Other action points for Allies include civil disobedience and acts of creative rebellion that have the potential to create social change, either incrementally or suddenly. Select your battle(s) carefully! Social media offers spontaneity in direct action, and to affect political reform we must practice an engaged civic activism. Allyship work includes honoring the treaties, making governments accountable, mobilizing resources, and taking action on addressing systemic racism and oppression everywhere it is found (in government, the legal system, the media, the commons, and within other social movements such as feminism). Solidarity has the potential to build bridges, and to renew relationships between native and non-native people, communities and nations.

Indigenous people have a long history of survivance and engagement in powerful decolonization strategies, and when we become Allies, we reject the ethics of hierarchy, capitalism, domination and eco-genocide that harm us all. First Nations worldviews that protect and revere the earth are still in place today, and by assisting them in their struggles for sovereignty, we are ensuring that precious watersheds, lands and ecosystems will be protected for all of us in *Earth Community*. Also, by sharing this *Beautiful Resistance* together (our "co-existence through co-resistance"), we automatically contribute to earth remediation and the healing of Turtle Island.

The founding documents of the Canadian and American nation-states mean that *We Are All Treaty* People, and on the path to peaceful co-existence with First Nations there are models to follow in reconciliation and wampum diplomacy. At this interface another exciting and holistic relationship is underway, a leading-edge "future-primitive" way to view indigeneity as intrinsic to the entire spectrum of human experience. By forming new subcultures and post-colonial "tribes," those of us of European descent are reawakening to the fact that we also have indigenous roots and ancestral traditions. And in this post-colonial era of massive change ("the great turning" or "paradigm shift") we are encouraged by many First Nations activists, leaders and academics to make this essential return. In our "Settler Re-landing" or "nativization," to follow the lead of First Nations people and relinquish our dominance in political, social and cultural life may be the most revolutionary ap-

---

10   There are many alternative narratives, but good starting points to revisionist history are *An Indigenous Peoples' History of the United States* by Roxanne DunbarOrtiz (Beacon Press, 2014), *A People's History of the United States* by Howard Zinn (Harper Perennial Modern Classics, 2010), *A Different Mirror: A History of Multicultural America* by Ronald Takaki (Back Bay Books, 2008), and *Conquest: Sexual Violence and American Indian Genocide* by Andrea Smith (South End Press, 2005). For a true history of the founding of Canada, *Clearing the Plains: Disease, Politics of Starvation, and the Loss of Aboriginal Life* by James Daschuk (University of Regina Press, 2013) recounts the politics of ethnocide that led to the deaths and subjugation of thousands of aboriginal people in the realization of Sir John A. Macdonald's "National Dream." These books illustrate that master narratives are a smokescreen disguising the conflict in the Americas between EuroEmpire and people of colour, whom they destroy, enslave, exploit and oppress.

A BEAUTIFUL RESISTANCE

proach of all!

Without romanticizing, misinterpreting or denying the holocaust that occurred in the Americas, it has been suggested that we can look to the original peoples to learn how to thrive, survive and flourish on Turtle Island, interconnected with the land and all life. After all, as outlined by Gustavo Esteva, everything we need for the paradigm shift is *"already in place as it has been for millennia, being lived by indigenous knowledge and indigenous people."*[11] We are being invited to learn from the First Peoples in whose territories we are now living, and to understand the traditional ecological knowledge (TEK) of our home landscapes in order to practice sustainability and relate to the environment properly.

From First Nations narratives and hands-on teachings we may discover that our homelands are a paradise rich in game, fish, native fruits, berries, nuts, seeds, vegetables, leaves, flowers, shoots, roots, herbs, barks, sap, grain, wild rice, insects, eggs, and other wild foods and medicine sources that contribute to our healing, health and well-being. These time-tested human and other-than-human interactions and practicalities of life on the land can give rise to lifeways, values and cultural keystones that become a living treasure for all. All the aspects of life we need to consider in a post-apocalyptic future will be determined by, or reinforced by, our interaction with the local environment, and the use of energy, food security, diplomacy, trade, defensive boundaries and customary law will all be physically defined by the existing watersheds and ecotones of our territory. Adopting an indigenous worldview means living lighter on the land, and building a society in which we never consume more than what we can replenish.

> After all, as outlined by Gustavo Esteva, everything we need for the paradigm shift is "already in place as it has been for millennia, being lived by indigenous knowledge and indigenous people."

The relational frameworks and Original Instructions that served Turtle Island First Nations for millennia prior to colonization are alive and thriving, perfectly intermeshed with localized landscapes and sustainable in today's world. In fact, pre-colonial indigenous knowledge may "be crucial to getting the human species out of the mess we now find ourselves in on Mother Earth."[12] Both native and non-native communities now share Turtle Island, and as we change our attitudes, alter our frameworks and revise our activities, the potential is there to find common ground in the recovery of our own ethnoculture(s) and earth-wise spiritualities.

It is clear that modelling our future after indigenous values is key to our rejection of Empire, and ancient knowledge combined with modern TEK in the revitalization of local community will enable us to survive the fast-approaching climate change crossroads. Re-centering indigenous values does not give us permission to appropriate the spiritual or cultural property of First Nations, but we are invited to embrace indigenous ethics such as reciprocity, balance,

---

11   Gustavo Esteva, Lecture, 2013 *Elders Conference*, Indigenous Studies Department, Trent University, Peterborough, ON, January 28, 2013.

12   Zainab Amadahy, "Why Indigenous and Racialized Struggles will Always be Appendixed by the Left," *Unsettling Settlers: Where We Talk about Unsettling Our Settler Selves*, 2012.

honesty, humility, love and kindness. It is enough to understand the basics of TEK and how it stems from the land, and then to focus on uncovering our own ancestral treasures. It may seem to be at cross-purposes to suggest that Pagans, Druids, Polytheists and Animists learn all they can about Turtle Island indigenous knowledge, but that is where a moral code comes in. To respect another culture with full knowledge of their TEK, without interfering, is what peaceful co-existence is all about. You are only an authority when it comes to your own ancestral knowledge, and as we come to understand cultural appropriation as another aspect of colonialism, we will steer clear of making that mistake.

Tragically, First Nations have only recently begun the recovery process from one apocalypse (the genocide, ethnic cleansing, oppression, racism, residential schools, loss of land and assimilation they experienced from our Settler-Colonial society) to be faced with another. Today, the destruction of the environment is the end result of our western knowledge system and a civilization far beyond its limits, leading to societal breakdown, economic chaos, extreme weather events and massive change. But our greatest hope is to realize that indigenous lifeways have already been in place for millennia on Turtle Island, and can continue for many more with a post-apocalyptic panoply of cultural wisdom practices, reciprocity worldviews and collaborations with the green world. We are living on Turtle Island – isn't it time we started acting that way? Our cultural recovery from Empire will go hand-in-hand with our efforts as Allies for the First Nations of this beautiful land as they continue to thrive, our convergence synonymous with social justice. For many of us - visionaries, soil tenders, new witches, green seers, wild women and crazy freedom fighters alike - activism on behalf of the Living Earth and equity for others has become the only path that matters.

Pegi Eyers

Author of Ancient Spirit Rising: Reclaiming Your Roots & Restoring Earth Community, Pegi Eyers is a Celtic Animist who sees the world through a spiritual lens, and is a devotee of nature-based culture and all that is sacred to the Earth. She is an advocate for the recovery of our authentic ancestral traditions, and lives near Nogojiwanong in Mississauga Anishnaabe territory. www.stonecirclepress.com.

Windsong

Lia Hunter

Mesa-top twilight smudges smoky sage around on the wind
Counter-world dreamtime seeping in, whistlings that round on the wind

Will you grasp and mark the rising tide of howling crescendo
Or be lost in noise of sprawl, pod, and team that pound on the wind

I once lost track of the medicine that I held so blithely
When a nightmare of wings hunted me, I was downed on the wind

Go tuck the holy broken things in the midden, and return
Lay low, the night spirits are screaming up the mound, on the wind

Come cast the water, the sand and salt, and make your circle bed
Relearning, shakingly, to rely on the ground, on the wind

Raining brings ancestors close to whisper what we always knew
Restoration, spirit life, memories that surround on the wind

Such songs sowed Kokopelli, forlorn flute soon to awaken
Call up the ancient new seductive healing sound on the wind

Windsong is written in the poetry form called the ghazal, and was inspired by the Navajo Night Chant,[13] which evokes the night winds/spirits that howl up the sides of the mesas as night falls... and haunts you until you sow it into a poem with other elements of the cultures of the Southwest of Turtle Island, a re-enchantment message from the ancestors, and a wink from Kokopelli.

Lia Hunter

Lia Hunter is an awenydd, anthropology major, and mother of two college students in Turtle Island's beautiful Mountain West. She writes for Gods & Radicals, SageWoman Blogs, and her blog, Awenydd of the Mountains. She strives to be a good ancestor.

13   (http://www.folkways.si.edu/musicoftheamericanindiansofthesouthwest/american-indian/album/smithsonian)

THE FIRE IS HERE

Sovereignty and the Trials of Love

Love and Possession of the Land

Heron

Beltane is a fertility festival when the May Queen walks through the enticing scents of flowers and the Horned God catches the scents and knows that the Summer has come. That's one way of experiencing it and one that can, and has, been enacted ritually. It sees the land performing its own rite of passion, described in human terms but occurring in the natural environment whether we are also in it or not. In more overtly human terms, the same scene can be enacted as a sovereignty ceremony, where a claim to rulership may be made by the act of 'marrying' the land over which rulership is claimed, and validated only by the acceptance of the sacred partner. In recorded history this tends to be a male king marrying the indigenous goddess of the land, but there is no reason why the relationship could not be one of a ruling queen marrying the god. Indeed in some Irish tales this does seem to be implied.

Lois Cordelia - Mythology and Folklore of the British Isles.

And for us, in the 21st century, what meanings can this have? For those of us whose relationship with the land is more than just aesthetic, and whose sense of possession is nothing to do with exclusive legal ownership, what relationship do we seek with the gods and the goddesses of the land? It may be felt with all the keenness of sexual attraction, cultivated with all the devotion of a deepening relationship and grow to a degree of love that is not unlike a marriage. Do married partners possess each other? Only figuratively, for no-one fully owns the being of another, though that being may be given over as an act of love. It is the same with the land. We may feel a sense of possession of 'my patch' - but it can never be exclusive as much as it may seem to be so at the point of contact within a relationship.

The Scottish poet Norman MacCaig has some verses about relationship with the land:

A BEAUTIFUL RESISTANCE

> Who owns this landscape?
> The millionaire who bought it or
> The poacher staggering downhill in the early
>   morning
> With a deer on his back?
>
> Who possesses this landscape?
> The man who bought it or
> I who am possessed by it?
>
> (from 'A Man in Assynt')

I say these lines are about relationship with the land, because that is the emphasis I want to make. But they are also about possession and ownership, and how that 'ownership' may be justified. Possession is, I think, the best word because it works both ways as MacCaig's verse indicates. You cannot possess land in its complete sense merely by having a legal right to it or as you might 'possess' a transient consumer object. Land is a subject, the starting point of the relationship, as much as it is the object that completes it.

Although I would not be averse to recognising a sense of ancestral rights here, this cannot apply in a merely dynastic way. If someone inherits land it may well be that a sense of ancestral birthright comes with the inheritance and even a sense of kinship with land that has always been 'part of the family'. But this cannot be exclusive. The 'lord' or legal owner may or may not have such a relationship with the land, as might a tenant farmer, or any other inhabitant of the area who has intimate knowledge of it. Those living on the land for generations inherit it as much as the legal owner does.

All this, though it may be disputed by some, seems to me to be indisputable. But what is more problematic is the sense in which someone might acquire this sense of possession after moving to an area from a different part of the country, or even from a different country entirely. How long does it take? One thing I am sure of: it comes as much from inside as it does from outside. It is a relationship rather than simply a matter of gaining familiarity with a new environment. Something *given* as much as something *taken*. I was not born or brought up in the village where I now live, though I have spent half of my life here and a lot longer living in the wider surrounding area. Feeling that I belong here took time and it was as much a matter of absorbing different cultural influences as becoming intimate with woods, mountains, rivers and streams. But having gained that intimacy I feel as much a part of the past here as I do of the continuity that leads into the future.

Incomers can become integrated - or not. There is an historical record that is part, too, of the legendary history of 'my' village. In the eleventh century a Norman baron called Walter de Bec built himself a small motte and bailey castle with a wooden tower on the site of a hill fort overlooking the valley. He had ventured further west in Wales than the Norman support network could sustain at that time and the castle was destroyed by locals and he eventually withdrew to his more secure estates in England. An englyn has been written about this in Welsh, using the native strict metre verse technique to commemorate his defeat, but also to warn that it is necessary to be on guard against his kind. I have written my own version of this englyn, not a literal translation but a verse using different imagery to convey the same idea:

> Into the close weave of our lives
>   came Walter
> A robber wasp in our hives;
> Long gone the day when his will thrives
> But his challenge still survives.

Who comes with a love for the land? And who comes with a lust for land? Each of these has an ap-

THE FIRE IS HERE

propriate response. But what of indifference? Unconscious neglect? Inhabiting the land in body though the spirit is elsewhere, in another land or - far worse - in no land at all. Perhaps living in cities makes the latter more likely, but in my experience the sensitive soul will respond to city areas, neighbourhoods, communities in the same way that I am talking about my own life in rural areas. But absentee landlords never know the land, the communities, the gods of the places they think they own. They can no more grasp their deep treasure than they can grasp the colours of a rainbow, nor any more lock them away as their personal possession.

We live in a time of mass migrations of people moving to lands which are very different from those they come from. Here I speak from a European perspective but those living elsewhere will know from their own times or from their history that these are common events. Migration is also our history even if further back in the past for some of us than for others. Whoever lived in Britain before the last Ice Age did not live here after it. Whatever settled attachments to the land were experienced over many generations by the hunter-gatherers of Europe in the Stone Ages, we know that the Bronze Age brought invasion, new settlement and cultural change, though at first it seems from the record of ancient DNA that it took many more centuries for these populations to mix. But eventually they did and out of the language(s) the invaders brought with them formed the earliest versions of Celtic, Germanic, Italic, Greek... etc, which record mythologies that survive in the historical record.

Did the gods move too, so that the peoples moving around also met them where they settled? And were the gods that came with them and the gods they encountered the same gods or did they find ways to integrate, to tolerate or to live apart from each other in parallel space? The mythological record contains many stories of gods as well as people integrating and/or separating out. But those others all remain embedded in the landscape we inhabit, or in a close but other space which, if our senses are tuned to it, we may see into. And so we know them too, those other folk under the hill, the lake or the woodland shade. They are our ancestors too, possessing and possessed by the land as much as people who consider they own it. Or they are strangers because we choose not to acknowledge them or their possession, but they consider that no denial of their birthright.

Who owns the land? We all do, and all of those others too. Would we share our love of the land? Yes. But those who disrespect what we share must be called to account and those who assert exclusive rights challenged. Love is absolute and scorns what would destroy the thing loved. The sovereignty stories of the past enact that relationship in terms of the social and cultural arrangements that prevailed then. For us sovereignty is shared, or challenged. The gods who confer it call upon us to respond and we have to find a way to validate that response for our own time, in our own places and with due ceremony. This is our task.

So, to end at our beginning, Beltane is a time of fertility, but also a time when the faerie realm is closest - or most open - to our own. In the version of this mythology which I am possessed by, the gates of Annwn open and Rhiannon, the Horse Goddess, comes clothed in enchantment to seek a mate. She comes to make the two lands one as she comes to be one with the husband she seeks. In this story she lifts a veil to reveal herself and so becomes part of our world. She embodies our love of our land, and of her land. After all, the love tryst as part

> Who comes with a love for the land? And who comes with a lust for land?

of the May Games is well established and it is not so far removed from the encounter with Faërie. Who holds sovereignty here? Not the legal authorities for all the power they wield. Those who hold possession are also those who are possessed, who know the old stories not as deeds of ownership but as the living breath that blows through this world from the Otherworld when the worlds meet and become one. This is more real than any legal contract, more true than any fiction of ownership. But we need to give it a shape in our social customs and bring it alive in our personal lives. May it be so.

Heron

Heron (Greg Hill) is a Brythonic Polytheist from Wales in the island of Britain. He is a poet, a remembrancer of the land's embedded memories and a celebrant of its living spirit. His researches into Brythonic lore bear fruit on his blog The Path of the Awenydd and on the web site Awen ac Awenydd. He is a devotee of Rigantona whom he knows more intimately as Rhiannon and has a web site of information about her: www.rigantona.net.

Geraldine Moorkens Byrne

Born 1968, Dublin, Republic of Ireland where she still resides with her husband and two sons. Poet, publisher, and author of one children's book, Geraldine has been published in a variety of media including printed collections, magazines and e-zines. Her work has been performed on radio and the stage. She writes about a wide variety of topics, their diversity unified by the influence of Old Irish poetic forms, Irish heritage and culture on her work. Using the old Gods and sagas she frequently addresses concerns of the modern age. Her first full collection of poems will be published by PPP Publishing in 2016.

Eriu Addresses the False Kings

Geraldine Moorkens Byrne

As the False Kings attempt to impost themselves on the people, Eriu moves from Her seat to address the assembled crowd

False speaker, false leader, false man
Born of a woman, unworthy of the honour
Debased by your rejection of Her womb, Her heart
Enemy to half the world
Apostate to the other
Liar and spreader of lies, like mould and decay
Dead among men, unborn among women
Unclean among the pure of spirit
Firenne rejects you
You are false and therefore unable to exist
You are the three marks on a king's cheek
Your ramparts fall before the anger of the Druids
And the Wise Women will make bread from the fire
Of your roof,
The earth rises against you
The stones and bones and blood of the land
Reject you and your band
Be they born of the land, they are undone
Found them shelter in this land, they are undone
If they visit this land, they are undone
The birds of the air, the food of the earth
The spirit of life, the Tuatha and their homes
The Tiarna and their laws, the Tír and its being
Turn from you, deny you, fast against you
The root of your name shall be poisoned in the ground
Your stem shall be blighted and the ground salted against you
Your tongues fall silent, your limbs weakened, your fruit die untasted on the branch
And you shall be unmourned in the hour of your fall.

THE FIRE IS HERE

"Giving Power, Taking Power:
Emotional Labor, Gender, and Abuse"

Sophia Burns

"...give a portion of your power to women..."
— Roman prayer to Cybele

Her legs buckle and I know what to do.

I don't just mean easing my client to the ground and checking for stroke. As I wait for the charge nurse, I focus on my smile. Other residents have visitors, after all; they're liable to complain about a caregiver who lets it show that she's had too little sleep for a 12-hour shift. Nursing resembles customer service, wait staffing, and retail: most of the work does not involve the specific set of tasks listed in the job description. 80% of the time, nursing means presenting cheerfulness, politeness, deference, and a willingness to handle other people's interpersonal tension no matter how they treat you.

And as I push through the minor crisis on the emotional momentum of my devotional prayer that morning, I wonder, "Why should my employer care about my facial expression as much as my ability to cushion this client's fall?"

Of course, it's gender.

Two sociologists in particular have defined the ways we approach the connections between gender, emotions, and work. Emerging from the Second Wave of Western feminism in the 60s and 70s, Louise Kapp Howe wondered whether increased access to paid work had, in fact, much improved women's lives.

She found that women overwhelmingly got shunted into low-wage, majority-women, service-sector occupations; for these she coined the term "pink-collar" (as opposed to still-male-dominated blue- and white-collar jobs).

Later, Arlie Hochschild's book *The Managed Heart* showed us what those pink-collar jobs disproportionately involve: she termed it emotional labor. Emotional labor is a waitress smiling and laughing even when a customer is rude. Emotional labor is a retail clerk greeting everyone who walks in with a smile, no matter how she actually feels. Emotional labor is a nurse aide acting pleasant even under deeply unpleasant conditions.

Emotional labor is the work of acting like you feel a certain way because the boss and customers demand it. And emotional labor, above all, is "women's work."

She tells me everyone thinks I'm disgusting and I know what to do.

This time it's not a client, but a partner. Relationship abuse, though often not discussed, is as much a reality for LGBT people as for straights. By this point, she'd quite effectively isolated me with a move across the country, and I wouldn't get away from her for sev-

A BEAUTIFUL RESISTANCE

eral more months. So I smile, and I draw on whatever emotional strength I can find - from the Meter Theon, from myself, from the ability to do emotional labor on demand that women under patriarchy have to develop. The skill set here didn't differ from the one I use at work. And in principle, it doesn't differ from the work of listening-with-empathy that I do for female and non-binary friends (who reciprocate it), and for male friends (who perform it neither for me nor for each other, getting it from women instead).

Women who've survived abuse often have people asking why we put up with it, why we stayed even after it became "really" bad. There's plenty of answers - lack of financial resources, absence of crucial support networks, nowhere to leave to - but I rarely hear the biggest reason of all. Satisfying other people's desires without expecting reciprocation is what women do; under patriarchy, that's what "women's work" means.

Much of the emotional labor required of pink collar workers involves smiling and apologizing at people targeting you with abusive behaviors. Tell an angry, verbally-violent customer, "don't talk to me like that. I deserve basic respect," and you'll likely get fired. Submitting to an abusive partner or family member involves precisely the same work, and it's work forced on most of us by the power structure of capitalism. The requirements of paid pink-collar work reinforce abusive dynamics at home, while the emotional conditioning of unpaid abuse makes women better at putting up with it on the job.

Capitalism runs on the abuse of women.

> **Patriarchy is the system growing on women's unpaid, unreciprocated work (emotional, domestic, and social). And like all exploitation, patriarchy harms its victims.**

"Religion is the sigh of the oppressed creature, the heart of a heartless world, and the soul of soulless conditions."

— Karl Marx

When faking happiness at work is more than my depressive brain can bear, I pray for strength and find that the Mother of the Gods answers. When tolerating my abuser without melting down became more than was possible, I also prayed for strength, and also found that the Mother answered. Sure, Marx may have opposed religion on principle. But I wouldn't have lasted this long without the power my goddess gives me. Patriarchy is the system growing on women's unpaid, unreciprocated work (emotional, domestic, and social). And like all exploitation, patriarchy harms its victims. Women are consistently more religious than men across many different traditions. This holds even truer for Paganism than for the Abrahamic religions Marx had in mind. We seek so much divine support because we can't keep going without it.

Many of us are used to getting through on the strength our deities give us, and many of our deities are used to "giving a portion of power to women" because women need it. But part of our work as anticapitalists involves removing the need for religion to act as a stopgap for exploited, struggling people. We humans deserve better, and our gods do too.

"Everybody wants a revolution, but nobody wants to do

THE FIRE IS HERE

the dishes."

— Shane Claiborne

In the left-wing subculture, certain roles and political strategies get glory. Everyone wants to admire the building occupier who stands firm when they get pepper sprayed, or the leader whose oratory whips a crowd of demonstrators into ecstasy, or the organizer who founded six organizations and sits on the steering committee for five more. Confrontation and "speaking truth to power" surely do take courage and express the righteous fury of the activist community; sometimes, they even get material results. But there's more to revolution than challenging the old (including the often-unsung behind-the-scenes work that allows confrontation to occur; while this work is disproportionately done by women, the visible glory-winning roles still tend to go to men). You also need to build the new.

During the Indian independence struggle, Gandhi developed a theoretical distinction between an "obstructive program" and a "constructive program." The former means challenging existing unjust systems and demanding they change (by whatever tactics one chooses; virtually everything activists in the US currently do falls into this category). The latter, however, means building something better now, so that when the old system falls, something will be ready to take its place. While we need both, Gandhi rightly prioritized the latter, saying: *"My real politics is constructive work."*

Patriarchy is about labor. Patriarchy is about exploitation. And without doing away with patriarchy, we won't really be able to undo capitalism; like all structures of exploitation, they're too mutually reinforcing to get rid of just one by itself. The type of work exploited through patriarchy is generally women's unwaged and unnamed domestic and/or emotional labor (be it in a pink-collar job or just informally, between friends, families, and lovers). Until you start looking for it, it's hard to notice; so is abuse, of course, and abuse exists on a spectrum with unreciprocated emotional work. We can't get rid of abuse without getting rid of the entire spectrum. Our constructive program must involve men doing this labor for each other and doing it for women. Even our male revolutionaries need to start doing the dishes.

Otherwise, women won't find our communities sharing power and support together. We'll only have what strength our gods can give.

Sophia Burns

Sophia Burns is a galla, vowed to serve Kybele and Attis, and a Hellenic polytheist. She writes for Gods & Radicals and the nonsectarian Left website The North Star, also serving on the latter's editorial board. She and her partners live in the Pacific Northwest of the United States.

All Hail the Runners
Hunter Hall

I used to believe that
the greatest act of love
was to sacrifice,
to be supple,
to bend like a bridge
to let you in
like I was inviting you to
tea, cake, everything.

Now that I am older
I understand that this is just
a lie told to young girls
by men of your ilk
to consume
possess and conquer
young girls,
turning them into old girls
and then throwing them away
if they do not run first.

I ran
I ran so fast
my lips blistered and my skin cracked
while your howls followed me
for years and years
proclaiming your love, hate and ownership of me,
attempting to reassert your control,
to claim your land.
My body is not acreage
and I am not what you failed to make me.
Promises made while the beast is hidden
Do Not Count
when locked in a tower

THE FIRE IS HERE

dressed in rags.
It took at least a quarter
to relearn to trust my voice

That is the hardest part.
I forgot I had a voice
because whenever I opened my mouth
your voice came out.

Do not listen to the pretty lies
that fall out of the lips
of those who wish
to hold your fire
only to put it out.

All hail the runners.

Hunter Hall

Hunter Hall's a ferocious poet seen late last century lurking black-hooded about the rainy streets of Seattle. Reading Deleuze & Guattari while slinging brutal mochas, channeling serpents and raw riot through her spoken-word performances, she now lurks somewhere in the Salish Sea, plotting revolution while baking for her children.

We Are The Rude:
Bourgeois Morality, False Commons, and Pagan Love

Rhyd Wildermuth

The feet should set perpendicular to the ground, the knees almost together. **It would be uncivil to stretch out the legs,** *or place one foot on top of the other. If you are in special company, do not cross your legs.*

Among friends of the same level, it is normal to do so.

— from **"A Catholic Manual of Civility,"** a primer used to educate Brazilian boys on how to act like Christians.

Picture with me a man I've seen quite often. He's large and sits on a bus, taking up several seats. He's got his legs spread out, one completely into the aisle. Also, to one side of him are several bags and a backpack. He's taking up a lot of room and doesn't seem to notice or care that others could be sitting in those spots. Worse, he's clipping his fingernails, and he's listening to loud music.

This man is engaged in manspreading. You're maybe aware of the concept—it's in the Oxford Dictionary now:

The practice whereby a man, especially one traveling on public transportation, adopts a sitting position with his legs wide apart, in such a way as to encroach on an adjacent seat or seats.

And the problem of 'manspreading' was significant enough to lead the MTA in New York to levy fines to men for spreading their legs, as well as posting signs stating, "Dude... Stop The Spread, Please."

If you ride public transit, you're probably recalling all the times you've sat next to some ass who's taken up too much space, or found yourself standing because there's no room. And maybe you agree with certain Tumblr blogs and internet memes that his callous disregard of others is an obvious display of The Patriarchy, because women either can't, don't, or wouldn't do such things.

Before we go on, though, I should tell you two things. The man I mentioned? He's Black and homeless. The bags he carries contain all of his human possessions. And he smells a bit different from the rest of the folks on the bus, 'unpleasant' to most people. And he mutters to himself. And he grooms himself, all things which are considered rude in public spaces. And we'll talk more about him later.

The second thing I should tell you? *I 'manspread' too.*

Why? It's not, as some ridiculous Men's Rights Advocates have suggested—and popular anti-manspreading Tumblr accounts have asserted—that I'm attempting to give more space to my genitals. Any man with testicles so large (and fragile) that sitting upright would crush them probably shouldn't be sitting at all. Nor is it because I think I deserve more space than others in cramped quarters.

There are actually two reasons I 'manspread.' The first reason may elicit a bit of sympathy from you and make you hate me a little less, and the second reason may give you a crucial key to understanding how Capitalism shapes all of our existences, creates social conflict, feeds racism, establishes The Patriarchy, and

THE FIRE IS HERE

ensures we fight each other rather than the rich.

Bear with me, yeah? And I'll try to give you a little more room here.

Work is Anti-Yoga

Mechanisation—the turning of the body, male and female, into a machine—has been one of capitalism's most relentless pursuits.

Silvia Federici—*In Praise of the Dancing Body*[14]

I was a chef for several years, working in quite a few restaurants in Seattle. Restaurants are Capitalist enterprises, and they're one of the best ways to see how the imperative for profit is always at war against the lives, desires, and bodies of workers.

At one of them, I fucked up my knee in the walk-in refrigerator. It was a very busy Friday night, and one of our servers asked me to move a keg for her. It wasn't 'my job,' but she was small-framed and didn't have the strength to move it, so I moved it for her. Unfortunately, I hadn't noticed that someone had spilled some water on the floor, and I slipped, contorting my leg so badly in the fall that my ACL (one of the ligaments which keeps the knee attached to the leg) snapped.

That hurt, by the way. A lot. And my bosses tried to fight my worker's compensation claim, which anyway wouldn't have paid for the $18,000 surgery I needed to replace the ligament. Fortunately, my partner at the time had just gotten a full-ride scholarship to grad school in Canada and I was able to come with him and get it fixed for free.

That surgery didn't fix the other problems that came along with the injury. I walk with a swagger now, my right foot is always askew from my left foot. The inclination of my body, when sitting in any sort of chair (except a straight-backed, wooden chair) is to slump forward to reduce the pressure on my lower back with my legs splayed. That is, I 'manspread,' but not because I'm a jerk: I'm actually trying not to experience significant pain.

I still try to compress myself as much as possible in tight situations, aware the experience of being in crowded spaces is uncomfortable for everyone. There's a calculus involved; is my pain likely greater or less than the discomfort someone sitting next to me might feel?

Most people can't claim this injury as an excuse, though. But plenty of people (mostly men) still do this, apparently clueless (or worse, unconcerned) about the experiences of others around them. Are there so many assholes in the world?

Maybe. But the language and ethics we use to understand and judge 'manspreading' or other 'anti-social behaviors' is pretty insufficient. For instance, it certainly can't be said that having one's knees spread open is The Patriarchy in action when we consider documents like the *Catholic Manual of Civility* (quoted at the beginning of this essay) or other Christian primers which were used to 'educate' poor and indigenous peoples into acting 'civilized.' After all, the Catholic Church is pretty much synonymous with Patriarchy.

So, what's going on with manspreading and our

> Restaurants are Capitalist enterprises, and they're one of the best ways to see how the imperative for profit is always at war against the lives, desires, and bodies of workers.

---

14   *A Beautiful Resistance #1: Everything We Already Are*, (Gods & Radicals, 2015), p 84

generally angry reactions to it? Let's go back to the kitchen where I hurt my knee, and I'll tell you another reason why I think most men 'manspread.'

That kitchen was poorly designed, like almost every restaurant in which I've ever worked. When building a restaurant, an owner is faced with a calculus the customers rarely see. Space is always a premium, especially in an urban setting, and because an owner wants to maximize profit, the dining area receives priority when deciding how the space will be set up.

The more tables available in a restaurant, the more customers can eat at once. More customers equals more profit for a restaurant owner, and under Capitalism, profit is the primary imperative. Thus, the more space devoted to customers, the more potential profit.

But the more space devoted to dining, the less space can be devoted to the kitchen and server-stations. Obviously, a restaurant requires a kitchen in order to operate, but more often than not, the kitchen is quite small. I've worked in quite a few excruciatingly small spaces, and applied for two jobs where, at 6 foot 1 inch and 200 pounds, I was told *"You're too big to work in our kitchen."*

Another thing about many of these kitchens—the counters are often a little too short if you're of above-average height. Counters on the line (where most of the preparation was done) are often slightly too short to work without slouching over, something my tall co-workers often complained about but something my shorter co-workers claimed never to notice. Shorter co-workers experienced other problems in these kitchens, though. Many shelves were often placed very high in order to maximize the use of space (sometimes so high that even I had trouble reaching them). One liked to think that the inconveniences, body-aches, posture problems, and other difficulties the taller workers experienced balanced out the same problems experienced by the shorter of us.

Besides, work is anti-yoga, right?

In all these cases, though, we workers needed to contort, squeeze, stretch or bend our bodies to fit the space allotted us. We had no control over the design of the kitchens (and definitely not the size), but ultimately faced the choice: transform our bodies to fit the work, or hope to find a place our bodies fit better.

Cramped, Crowded, and Capitalist

My experience in kitchens initiated me into an understanding of the conflict between space and profit-imperative. And my experience with my knee injury led me to understand a bit more about the design of public spaces, particularly in transportation.

In Capitalist societies, public transit operates under the same profit-imperative that affects workspaces, even if there's no money being made. Costs must be kept to a minimum, revenue must be maximized, and accommodation of human bodies is often an afterthought (if thought about at all). Calculations are made to ensure the least amount of buses or trains are run on routes to move the largest amount of people, keeping labor cost (bus-drivers, mechanics, etc.) down, and human difference is an unfortunate

> In Capitalist societies, public transit operates under the same profit-imperative that affects work-spaces, even if there's no money being made.

problem to be overcome, not a primary logic.

The seats in public transit are standardized—that is, the same seat is available to a person who is 6'5" as someone 4'10". In a situation where all seats were built large enough to accommodate a very tall person, everyone would likely be quite comfortable (particularly those for whom such seats would mean a lot of extra room). But, of course, this is not the case. Designing such spaces for very tall people would reduce the amount of available space, increasing the overall cost while decreasing the potential profit (excess revenue) from transit riders.

If you are tall and find yourself sitting in a seat too short for you, your knees either hit the seat in front of you or are a little higher than your waist. The first problem is quite painful after just a minute or two (try pressing your kneecap against a wall for a couple of minutes and describe the feeling), while the second situation puts quite a bit of pressure on your lower back and spine (try this by sitting in a chair, putting a few books under your feet so your knees are slightly higher than your waist, and feel where it starts to hurt).

In both cases, widening the distance between your knees relieves the pain. That is, splaying your legs ('manspreading') is one way the body tries to fit in a space not designed to fit it. In fact, this position could be said to be the body attempting *to act like a body*, rather than a machine.

But let's consider what else the Capitalist logic of standardization of space and disregard for human difference does. The situation for those in wheelchairs is awful. On most buses in the cities where I've lived, there's often only 2 spots available for them. These spots are also the same spaces allotted to the elderly, blind, or otherwise impaired. On top of this, women with children in strollers, homeless folk with handcarts, or travelers with luggage must compete for these same spots, and a hierarchy arises to determine who is most 'deserving' of the space.

I've watched a tragic number of fights between harried single mothers with children and elderly folks over that last remaining seat, and unsuprisingly, they are often of different skin colour. Worse, support and intervention from other passengers tends to fall along racial and class lines, too, a pitched social battle to determine which vulnerable person should be favored over another.

The scarcity of space and disregard for human difference generates strife and conflict, as is the potential for all scarcity. But let's look at another aspect of this scarcity of space to find the answer to a question very few ever seem to ask.

There's Only One Thing Between Us

I recently returned from a week visiting my sisters, and had the delightful pleasure of sitting in between two financial managers who were taller—and wider—than I on a flight with an ultra-low-cost airline. You can perhaps imagine the experience. Middle-seats are already uncomfortable, whether you're tall or not. Add to this my posture issues from the aforementioned knee problems and the fact that all three of us were too large for the seats in which we sat. Figure in to this that airlines have increasingly reduced the distance between rows of seat, and you've got an unpleasant experience altogether.

Airplanes, particularly, seem to generate their own realms of conflict. On a flight to Ireland from Orlando a year ago, I watched a woman hit an older man repeatedly with her carry-on luggage and shout at him when he asked her to be more careful. It looked almost like it'd come to fists, the woman becoming increasingly belligerent and threatening, her antagonism increasing the more the old man insisted she stop hitting him. And others were starting to take sides, and it was awful.

Of course, we were all cramped. We had all passed

through intrusive security measures in an airport which treats humans less like people and more like cattle being led to market. We all had an impending 8-hour flight in an enclosed steel tube. The seats were small, the overhead compartments hardly designed to ensure it was easy to put things in and take things out. Though the woman was being quite awful to the old man, I couldn't deny she was reacting to the stress of the space and the utter lack-of-control any human must endure when traveling by air.

Put a bunch of people in a tiny cage for 8 hours and they're likely to act out, yes? But since we're talking about standardized space and the Capitalist profit-motive, it's particularly worth looking at the cold war that occurs in every seat over the arm rest. If you're in the middle, you've got it worst—the person on your left and your right are likely to dominate the armrest to either side of you, and you are faced with the choice: force your way to a little more comfort, or stew for the duration about the assholes on either side of you?

But wait—there's an obvious problem here we take for granted (if we even notice at all):

Why is there only one arm-rest between two seats???

It's certainly not that chairs come with only one arm rest, nor that it's impossible for seat-makers to make them large enough that two people could put their arms there.

The reason, again, is Capital. To give each person enough room to move and to rest their arms without struggling against another person would require larger seats, and gaps between them. Doing so would run directly counter to the imperative of the Capitalists who profit from air-travel. In fact, to sit in comfortable seats where you are not compelled to battle in a long war of 'micro-aggressions' with the people next to you requires paying an extreme premium to sit in 'first class.'

Here we can finally see the crux of the problems we face in public places. All those petty conflicts, all those micro-aggressions, and all the hierarchies which arise between people in crowded theaters, airplanes, public transit, and elsewhere arise in response to the conditions created by Capital.

The Body Is a Very Rude Thing

Rude: late 13c., "coarse, rough" (of surfaces), from Old French ruide (13c.) or directly from Latin rudis "rough, crude, unlearned."adj. perhaps related to rudus "rubble." Sense of "ill-mannered, uncultured; uneducated, uncivilized" is from mid-14c.

Rural: early 15c., from Old French rural (14c.), from Latin ruralis "of the countryside," from rus (genitive ruris) "open land, country," from PIE *reue- (1) "to open; space" (see room (n.)). In early examples, there is usually little or no difference between the meanings of rural and rustic, but in later use the tendency is to employ rural when the idea of locality (country scenes, etc.) is prominent, and rustic when there is a suggestion of the more primitive qualities or manners naturally attaching to country life. [OED]

Rustic: mid-15c., from Latin rusticus "of the country,

since we're talking about standardized space and the Capitalist profit-motive, it's particularly worth looking at the cold war that occurs in every seat over the arm rest.

THE FIRE IS HERE

rural; country-like, plain, simple, rough, coarse, awkward," from rus (genitive ruris) "open land, country" (see rural). Noun meaning "a country person, peasant" is from 1550s (also in classical Latin). Related: Rustical (early 15c.).

Pagan: *late 14c., from Late Latin paganus "pagan," in classical Latin "villager, rustic; civilian, non-combatant" noun use of adjective meaning "of the country, of a village," from pagus "country people; province, rural district," (by extension, pejorative). Savage, immoral, uncivilized, wild.*

The imperative to profit leads an airline to cram as many people into as small a space as possible, just as business owners and other Capitalists expect workers to adapt their bodies in order to earn a living. The imperative to keep costs down means seats in public transit and other places are not large enough to accommodate the wide range of human size and mobility difference.

None of this excuses wretched behavior in public spaces: there's rarely any good reason to hit an old man with your valise, nor to prevent others from sitting by splaying your legs and laying out your bags. We still have expectations of public behavior and preferences against people being rude to us, strangers or otherwise.

But what passes for morality and civics (either amongst the codes of social justice or traditionalism) will always meet a dead end if the very conditions which create the conflict are ignored, dismissed, or denied. Worse, many of these concepts of morality and civics aren't even our own, anyway, but have been shaped by the constant need of the rich to have better-behaved and better self-disciplined workers.

The Birth of Bourgeois Morality & The War on The Rustic

"...the violence of the ruling class was not confined to the repression of transgressors. It also aimed at a radical transformation of the person, intended to eradicate from the proletariat any form of behavior not conducive to the imposition of a stricter work discipline. The dimensions of this attack are apparent in the social legislation that, by the middle of the 16th century was introduced in England and France..."

Silvia Federici, ***Caliban & The Witch*** (p.136)

Since the birth of Capitalism, humans have been increasingly compressed together into urban spaces because that is where most work is to be found. We should remember, though, that the people who filled the cities were often displaced people unaccustomed both to city life and particularly to factory life. In fact, it has taken centuries for factory owners (Capitalists) to train rural, peasant and 'uncivilized' peoples to endure the conditions of those factories.

On top of this, the peasants who came to the cities had been otherwise ungoverned. They were literally *un-civilized* and *un-disciplined*, and this made them very difficult to rule. The process of turning those people into what we have become now (that is, workers) was long, bloody, and involved altering the conditions of society itself so that the behaviors, patterns, man-

> It's taken centuries for those factory owners (capitalists) to train rural, peasant and 'uncivilized' peoples to endure the conditions of those factories.

A BEAUTIFUL RESISTANCE

ners—basically, *civilization*—required of those uncultured, unwrought, undisciplined people became not just part of the requirements of employment, but the actual basis of society.

The class of owners who needed disciplined workers? They're called the Bourgeoisie ('those in the city'). That 'Class Struggle' that Marx wrote about between the workers and the Bourgeoisie wasn't just pitched-battle, strikes, and police murder, but also a long period of shaping the behaviour of the poor (through laws, education, punishment, and public shaming) until the poor finally internalized that behaviour that would make them good workers.

This is the process Silvia Federici wrote about in **Caliban & The Witch: Women, the Body, and Primitive Accumulation,** and it included the eradication of the belief in magic:

"Eradicating these practices was a necessary condition for the capitalist rationalization of work, since magic appeared as an illicit form of power and an instrument to obtain what one wanted without work, that is, a refusal of work in action. "Magic kills industry," lamented Francis Bacon, admitting that nothing repelled him so much as the assumption that one could obtain results with a few idle expedients, rather than with the sweat of one's brow...

Magic, moreover, rested upon a qualitative conception of space and time that precluded a regularization of the labor process. How could the new entrepreneurs impose regular work patterns on a proletariat anchored in the belief that there are lucky and unlucky days, that is, days on which one can travel and others on which one should not move from home, days on which to marry and others on which every enterprise should be cautiously avoided?" (p. 142)

...as well as a complete change in the relationship of humans to the body:

It was in the attempt to form a new type of individual that the bourgeoisie engaged in that battle against the body that has become its historic mark. According to Max Weber, the reform of the body is at the core of the bourgeois ethic because capitalism makes acquisition "the ultimate purpose of life," instead of treating it as a means of the satisfaction of our needs; thus, it requires that we forfeit all spontaneous enjoyment of life (Weber 1958: 53). Capitalism also attempts to overcome our "natural state," by breaking the barriers of our natural state by lengthening the working day beyond the limits set by the sun, the seasonal cycles, and the body itself, as is constituted in pre-industrial society. (p.135)

That is, the process of creating the working class involved disciplining, taming, and civilizing people, stripping them both of their relationship to magic and particularly their relationship to the natural world, including to their own bodies. Or put another way, Capitalists required workers who had lost their rustic, rude, and rural qualities, which included their Pagan tendencies.

To do this, they got plenty of help from Christian leaders (John Wesley, the founder of Methodism, was one of their primary weapons in England) and other moralists who would help inculcate new social codes and norms into the unwashed, uncultured, rude poor. And as the Bourgeoisie continued to gain power, the

> Capitalists required workers who had lost their rustic, rude, and rural qualities, which included their Pagan tendencies.

scourge of rudeness, uncivilized behavior, and 'immorality' amongst the poor became an increasing topic of discussion. Primers of all sorts arose, aimed primarily at women and the poor to teach them how to act better, more polite, more like them.

Bourgeois Morality & Social Policing

While the war between the upper classes and the unwashed masses upon whom they relied was always being waged in Europe since the beginning of Capitalism, it got particularly intense in the early 20th century as very rich industrialists needed to find even more disciplined workers for their assembly lines. Henry Ford instituted a 'morality police' to monitor the personal lives of his workers, and John D. Rockefeller created an educational foundation to shape and advise government in creating better workers. From one of the position statements of that foundation:

"In our dreams, people yield themselves with perfect docility to our molding hands. The present education conventions of intellectual and character education fade from their minds, and, unhampered by tradition, we work our own good will upon a grateful and responsive folk.[15]

15   From the affably named, *"The Country School of To-Morrow In Which Young And Old Will Be Taught in Practicable Ways How to Make Rural Life Beautiful, Intelligent, Frutiful, Recreative, Healthful, and Joyous,"* by Frederick T Gates (Chairman of the General Education Board), 1913

Though many of these efforts took on the shape of benevolence (or paternalism), taken together they show that our actions, our self-discipline, and much of our morality has been shaped by the rich, not by our own self-generated ideas of what makes one a 'moral' person.

Again, what we should also give attention to here is that this is the same logic that comprised the *'white man's burden'* or the *mission civilatrice* of European missionaries, entrepreneurs, and civil servants in colonies on the African, Asian, and South American continents. The rhetoric used by wealthy industrialists towards 'white' poor people echoes exactly the rhetoric of paternalistic education of the 'uncivilized' peoples an earlier generation of Bourgeois needed to shape and mould through education and punishment.

We have inherited a system of morality that is not our own, but rather those of our rulers. We've been shaped and molded into a class of people who have internalized the morality of the Bourgeoisie and made it our own, while being alienated from our own bodies, the cycles of nature, and older beliefs in magic. This is, at least partially, the unacknowledged and rotten root of much of our tendencies to belittle and even hate those with disabilities (they are not 'good workers'), the very poor (they are rude, unhygienic, lazy—all anti-bourgeois traits), the messy (consider the popularity of voyeuristic shows about 'hoarders' in US television), and all manner

> We've been shaped and moulded into a class of people who have internalized the morality of the Bourgeoisie and made it our own, while being alienated from our own bodies, the cycles of nature, and older beliefs in magic.

A BEAUTIFUL RESISTANCE

of other 'anti-social' behaviours.

Moralism has quite the history of creating social conflict. As Hannah Arendt has pointed out, many moral codes and associated ideologies are rarely adopted by the powerful unless they are useful for governing. Race-theory (a relatively new ideology—there was no real notion of racial difference before the Enlightenment, and certainly not one inhabiting the general opinions of commoners) became useful as a governing ideology only when the rich needed to keep slaves and former slaves from uniting with European-immigrant workers against their bosses. Anti-Semitism is another such (im)moral code: a reliable trick of rulers and the rich in Europe was to whip up anti-Jewish sentiment amongst the poor and workers, just as Federici shows occurred against women.

In all these cases, it's quite difficult for us to see what is actually shaping our own morality, standards, and ideologies. This is hardly any excuse for being awful to people, of course, only a reminder that our ethical systems are too often inhabited by an almost invisible, almost Archonic, spirit of morality.

Let's return to the question of the so-called manspreader now. The person taking up too much space on a bus is not playing along with the rules of the space, but what are those rules, and who sets them?

We experience those spaces as 'community' spaces, but they aren't actually created by us, nor do we actually have control over them. This is more obvious in an airplane where it's easier to see that the passengers are not a community, but only temporarily stuck in the same space together. Public transit seems more like a communal space, but who actually controls them? Not the people who ride them or use them, except in very, very indirect ways like voting. And voting, anyway, only gives the illusion of influence, not actual say in any matter.

Someone preventing another from sitting in a seat is certainly being awful. But what they are doing is not much different from many of the other anti-social behaviors which have been criticized in the past by the rich. Rustic, rude, uncivilized, 'low-class' qualities: being loud, eating in public, grooming, having 'unruly' children, breastfeeding in public—all of these are the sorts of activities the poor and 'undisciplined' traditionally engage in, activities they have not been disciplined, educated, and socialised against.

That last aspect is most relevant to the question of 'manspreading' and other misplaced 'social-justice' crusades, because socialisation against unacceptable behaviors is most effective when it's performed by people within the same economic class as the offender. If the rich were to be going about telling women or men how to act in public spaces, disobedience of these standards would approach open revolt. But fortunately for them, we police each other, particularly through public shaming.

Since manspreading has been taken up as part of a Bourgeois Feminist critique and prescribed a heavy-dose of public shaming, we should recall two previous social menaces which attempted to bring men in line with proper social behavior: Prohibition, and the public shaming of war-resisters by women—including Suffragists—during World War I with white feathers.

Lest anyone misunderstand my point (and missed my heavy reliance on Federici here), let me be clear: the metrics and narratives of Feminism are crucial to any revolutionary understanding of our social conditions. Patriarchal forms persist and are the dominant ruling ideology within Capitalism, and none of this should be used an excuse to undermine truly radical Feminism.

But we should be particularly wary of the tendency to adopt Bourgeois Morality within our attempts to right the systemic wrongs caused by Capitalism, particularly when we find ourselves suddenly taking positions on questions that further oppress people whose very bodies stand as resistance to Bourgeois demands. Thus, Feminist leaders (for instance) who find themselves employing violent anti-trans rhetoric as part of their hopes to eradicate The Patriarchy are only helping Capitalism: the transperson, if anything, embodies a physical resistance to the Bourgeois need to divide the working classes into easily-managed categories.

Moreso, we must remember that a great many of the complaints about anti-social or 'rude' behaviors are directed toward the poor, homeless, people-of-color, immigrants, and others who are traditionally the enemies of Capital and the Bourgeoisie, and precisely whom any revolutionary project must not only include, but be led by. Anything which polices their behavior and reinforces 'respectability,' work-discipline, and Bourgeois moral standards must be rejected.

The Revolt of the Rude

None of this is to say that there is no place for morality or standards of social behavior. Nor is this to assert that Patriarchal attitudes do not persist in the behavior of men in public spaces. On the contrary, I'd argue that we actually cannot attack The Patriarchy, nor create community standards, without first attacking the problem of Bourgeois Morality and the illusory society it creates.

When someone's actions prevent us from using or enjoying a space, we feel wronged. This is an essential feeling, and one we ought to cultivate. In fact, it's precisely the feeling which fueled widespread resistance to Capitalism, Enclosure, and the creation of private property (land).

Before Capitalism, land was shared by a community who could use it as they saw fit, but custom, tradition, and social pressures kept them from over-using it. Over-hunting or over-harvesting in a forest, over-grazing or over-fishing in fields and streams meant the entire community suffered. The logic of The Commons was one of shared resources and shared obligations, and those who tried to 'squat' or 'enclose' shared spaces for themselves would be ostracized by the community.

But that older, rustic morality has been replaced by Bourgeois Morality. We now castigate the woman with too many shopping bags or the man with splayed legs on a subway while ignoring or even rewarding and praising the developer who turns open fields or run-down buildings into condos.

A person with their legs splayed, or their shopping bags filling the seats next to them, or the person apparently callous and indifferent to the needs of others in public spaces is violating the same sorts of societal standards which once held together The Commons, except for one difference: these are not The Commons. Our sense of fairness, of charitable social interactions, and our expectation that others around us will not 'take too much' linger, but the social spaces where such morals matter actually don't exist.

An airplane, a restaurant, a park, and even public transit in a Capitalist society are nothing like The Commons, because there is no real or direct community control over the size, shape, design, or use of those spaces. Instead, we have become like

> do we rush to judgment specifically because he reflects back to us our own imprisonment in the Capitalist work-ethic and Bourgeois Moralism?'

caged and severely disciplined animals punishing each other for taking up too much space in an increasingly Enclosed world, believing the illusion of our jailers, parroting their moral codes, mistaking proximity to community.

We should consider the man I mentioned at the beginning of this essay again. The Black homeless man on the bus, with his legs spread apart and his bags on the seat next to him, unshowered, cleaning his nails, talking loudly to himself and listening to a radio without headphones: is his behavior on account of poor upbringing (the conservative answer), male privilege (the pseudo-feminist answer), systemic injustice (the 'Social Justice' answer), his Blackness (the racist answer), or his homelessness (the Liberal and Capitalist answer)?

What if we rush to judgment specifically because he reflects back to us our own imprisonment in the Capitalist work-ethic and Bourgeois Moralism? What if it is only our own submission to the centuries-long moralistic training of the capitalist classes that makes us think we have the right to police his behavior in the first place, or even that there's anything wrong at all with what he's doing in a public space?

And what if he is actually showing us the gate to our own liberation?

I should here admit: it is hardly an easy journey through that gate. My own reactions to this man I mentioned embarrass me to no end, but I'll admit them, because you've probably felt some version of them, too. I'd often encounter him on days I really didn't want to go to work. He'd slow the bus down, take a long time to get on and an even longer time to disembark. He had a broken, swollen foot which extended far into the aisle, and it was never easy for people to get past him. And he smelled. It was evident he rarely showered, rarely washed his clothes. And though I am a social worker who regularly works with people with poor hygiene, his existence frustrated me.

No. He didn't just frustrate me, he annoyed me, and I obsessed over him. I'd blame him for making me late. I'd be irritated by his music. The sound of him clipping his nails pissed me off. When it was cold or raining, his body odor really made me angry, because I couldn't open the windows.

I wasn't the only one, either. An awful camaraderie develops between people sharing a mutual annoyance at 'anti-social' behavior. Women and men, all of them white and well-dressed, rolled their eyes and held their nose and made other signs to each other, sharing an imagined solidarity of suffering in the presence of this human. You've seen this, I know. You've been part of it. We all have.

If anything, though, I almost *hated* him, because he made me confront the very real conditions of my own life. He and I are both subjects of Capitalism, but I'm luckier. I had a job, had a home, could go to a bar or buy a latte as my reward for being a good worker, for doing what I'm supposed to do. He had no home or job, no place to shower, no place to store his stuff, no private place to clip his nails or listen to music without anyone judging it.

He was me, or me if I didn't obey.

More than that, though, he didn't have to worry about all the internalized fear about his public presence. He didn't bother compressing his body into a tiny space, he gave no regard to how much stuff he was carrying in public. He was free to enjoy music in public without giving a shit what other people thought, and

> He (and not I) was the true Pagan, the rustic, rural, rude remainder of Capitalist civilization

he'd laugh off (or sometimes just say 'fuck you') to anyone who'd ask him to turn it down. I think I was a little envious of him—not his poverty or homelessness, but his freedom from the regime of Bourgeois respectability and hatred of the body in all its rustic, unwrought, uncivilized, and unapologetic glory.

But more than anything, he reminded me that all the freedoms and luxuries and comforts that I 'earned' as a good worker came with the sacrifice of my soul and the internalization of the very logic which causes him to be homeless. I'd start thinking about how much I'd rather not be going to work, and how uncomfortable the tiny seat into which I'd crammed myself, with my knees pressed hard against the seat back in front of me, was.

And I'd start thinking about my illusion of control and the false 'community' I'd let myself believe I was a part of. I didn't know anyone on these buses, and they weren't created with people my size in mind, nor were they really 'socialist.' They existed to help ensure workers could get to their jobs, because without them Capitalists would have trouble finding workers to exploit.

The man before me was the Abyss into which any of us must stare, if we are ever to hope to lose our chains and become free. He (and not I) was the true Pagan, the rustic, rural, rude remainder of Capitalist civilization, and the price he paid for his freedom was homelessness, poverty, and the hatred of the rest of us on the bus.

Manifesto of the Rude

We can, of course, allow things to remain as they are, instituting increasing rules and public-shaming crusades against people who don't act civilized. The rewards for doing so are waged out in hours and shiny products, evenings at restaurants and weekends at bars.

We can even convince ourselves that we are doing some good, fighting The Patriarchy or making a more socially just society by policing each other, making sure we act in-line, keep our heads down, and never let our bodies be anything but efficient machines to be tucked-away and put out of sight after use.

Or, we can revolt, reclaiming the rudeness of our bodies, refusing to apologize for the amount of space we take up, our difference in size and shape and ability. But to do so requires a sort of decolonization and an overthrow of the Bourgeois Morality which has shaped what we believe to be polite, civil, and good.

What would such a morality look like? What would be our demands?

We could start by refusing the easy answers in uncomfortable situations. Instead of demanding that others follow the rules we've internalized, we should interrogate those rules and our reactions to the bodies of others. Are they really doing us harm, or are we actually struggling against our own desires for liberation?

We could also start by demanding an end to the Capitalist logic of standardization. If a body doesn't fit in a space created by Capitalist logic, it's not the fault of the body. We should stop demanding others squeeze themselves into such spaces, and demand there be more room to be human. This is particularly essential in regards to those with disabilities.

Likewise, we should stop pretending that public spaces are anything like The Commons. It is not the person taking up too much space in a bus or train who is the enemy, it is the rich who own the land under our feet. This would be the first step to reclaiming actually-existing Commons, land shared by communities where the poorest amongst us can subsist outside the imperative of Capitalist work.

And finally, we must embrace all that is rude and rustic about others in order to liberate our own bodies. As noted by Federici in her reference to Max Weber, Capitalism requires us to see our bodies as means to gain wealth while forfeiting spontaneous enjoyment. Therefore, leisure, frivolity, and celebration must not only be part of our resistance, but the foundation of our morality. Rather than shame (or worse—report) the person brushing their hair or eating food in a bus, shouldn't we rather delight in such things? Are they not caring for their body the way the rest of us do? Couples engaged in public displays of affection—is there not something beautiful—and Pagan—about people expressing love? Or the rude person playing loud music on a bus, what if we danced to that music or sang along? Is there anything more Pagan than music in a public space?

If anything, such a revolt of the Rude would also be a revolt of love. Love would cause us to demand more space for ourselves, more enjoyment of our bodies. Love would stand against the logic of the machine and the shaming of the stranger. Love would claim the right to live outside the demands of profit. Love would make us bodies again, rather than workers.

Love is a very, very rude thing.

Let's be in love.

Rhyd Wildermuth

Rhyd Wildermuth lives by the Salish Sea in occupied Duwamish territory. He's an anarchist, bard, and theorist, a columnist for The Wild Hunt and managing editor of Gods & Radicals. He laughs when he's happy, cries when he's sad, growls when he's thinking, and does all those things when he is in love. His work can be found at Paganarch.com

LOVE LETTER / CARTA DE AMOR
Simcha Bensefis

Solstice is coming and I want to see you
Dancing like you did that night in Montana

I am practicing being alone
I am forever grateful for loving myself

I'm not the machinery that alienates you
Nor was it anything I wrote

The chilli is bubbling on the stove
I'm waiting by the door and

Remember last year?
We were blasting rancheras y norteño in the most important ways, so
Who wants to free someone else?

Sailor Pluto rules over my summer months
They're eating chicken and I'm looking around at the botanica for you

Nightflight to Missoula and then we need to say goodbye
I'm wearing those pentagram earrings, porque tenía una cita con mi gente

I dream of oceans,
Churning salt water, 75%:
I am healing up

Return to where you came from:
Please, come voice yourself.

Simcha Bensefis

Simcha is a rad non-binary QPOC brujx, community activist & voodoo devotee living on occupied Kalapuya & Chinook territory. By day they work in community mental health & by night they can be found spinning in circles & dreaming of faraway desert lands.

A BEAUTIFUL RESISTANCE

A Forest Allegiance

NICOLAS GUY WILLIAMS

Nicolas Guy Williams (1970-) studied Fine Art at Cardiff, Wales 1989-1992. Lived in France for 10 years and is a Post post modernist Poet/Writer/Artist and Philosopher currently investigating Magic Realism and eco-shamanic poetic and prose experiment with the aim of developing shamanic realism as a literary tradition.

Woman of the Sap
Nicolas Guy Williams

from tree heart to tree top
I stretch and flow
leaf pale and leaf new
my hair knows

through sap I sing
through twig and branch and rugged bark
not to touch your mind
but instead your heart

I am the bare branch
the green lichen and
the silver paper of that birch
whispers as my hand

underneath the delving soil
my roots contend
following the forest folk
until their journey ends

be gentle in
my realm and I
will shelter you
from falling rain and sun filled sky

take not
live branch from my dress
lest tree falls across your path
to shake your heart and stop your step

Plant Magic

Sean Donahue

Like gods and people, plants exist for themselves -- and as part of the complex ecologies from which they emerge. Many contemporary magical practitioners approach them simply as inert objects to be used in ritual or spellcraft -- a perspective and approach that both emerge from and reinforce capitalist materialist culture's denial of the living intelligences of the other than human world. Far richer, more powerful, and more revolutionary magic comes from engaging plants as allies.

The Men Who Sold the World

"We must have died alone, a long long time ago." —David Bowie

When and how did plants become mere material for the fulfilment of human needs and desires? To some extent the process began with the birth of civilization, but it was completed in the bloody birth of capitalism.

Capitalism was born of tremendous violence -- the forced displacement of the western European peasantry, genocide and ecocide throughout the Americas, and the kidnapping, murder, enslavement, and exploitation of millions of Africans. The collective trauma of this violence created a collective dissociation, a psychic numbing that distanced many of its survivors and their descendants from the emotional impact of past and ongoing brutality. The alienation that characterizes life under capitalism arises from that violence and helps to perpetuate it.

As English and French philosophers and scientists began to articulate a new vision of the world, a paradigm arose with and from capitalism that served to erase most of the remnant elements of animism and communitarianism from European (and the emerging colonial North American) culture where, prior to the enclosures, they still maintained a degree of influence in both daily and ritual life in rural communities despite the best efforts of church and state. The local economics of mutual aid were replaced by a model that saw individuals acting in their own narrowly defined self interest as the economy's primary actors. Simultaneously, medicine shifted from a context in which a person who cultivated deep relationships with other than human realms made offerings, petitions, and agreements on behalf of a person who was suffering, in order to restore balance in microcosm and macrocosm to one in which technicians who held specialized knowledge performed precise interventions on the inner workings of bodies that were seen as identical machines. Like the human body, the world itself began to be seen and treated more like clockwork than like a living, fluid system with an animating intelligence of its own.

The alchemy of the sixteenth century was rooted in a cosmology that saw the material world as an imperfect and fallen representation of what the Christians' god intended it to be, and sought to find the process by which a thing could be reified into its essence. In the seventeenth century, that cosmology degenerated into one in which the world was made up of resources waiting to be reified into wealth. Human lives were viewed no differently from anything else in either cosmology. In the Christian mysticism that underlay European alchemy, humans were seen as sinners who through the pursuit of wisdom could attain a gnosis that would imbue grace. In capitalism's more toxic mimic of that world view, stretches of time of human lives could be bought for money and become instruments of productivity that would yield wealth to the men who bought them.

How else would other than human lives be viewed in such a paradigm than as resources that could be extracted and refined to yield value -- primarily as foods and medicines whose forms would become more and more distant from those of the plant bodies that yielded them as capitalism advanced, until, under late capitalism, corn syrup became liquid gold capable of producing sufficient wealth to buy elections, and most medicines ceased being made from recently living plants at all, instead becoming simulacra of plant molecules crafted from the fossil remnants of long dead ancient life.

Instrumental Plant Magic

As much as it represented a challenge to it, and a resurgence of some of the aspects of human life destroyed and suppressed by it, the magical revival of the later half of the last century emerged from within the culture that commodified the world. And as much as recent generations of Pagans and Polytheists have spoken and written about the sacredness of all life and the re-enchantment of the world, many contemporary texts, teachings, and practices involving plant magic treat herbs as tools in a ritual or a spell, and base their sense of a plant's role in the work at hand on memorized correspondences rather than on any direct relationship with plants themselves.

Pagandom has too often also been complicit in the New Age appropriation, distortion, and commodification of plants with whom Indigenous people have long and deep magical and ceremonial relationships.

White Sage, *Salvia apiana,* is a case in point. Based on a limited and decontextualized understanding of the ritual cleansing practices of some of the Indigenous peoples of what we now call southern California, many people who have no direct experience of the living plant burn it to clear a space or prepare for a ritual. The overharvest of White Sage for commercial smudge sticks has decimated wild populations of the plant and disrupted the ability of people whose families and communities have worked with *Salvia alpina* for thousands of years to maintain their connection with the plant.

To be sure, White Sage produces a beautiful smoke. Hir scent stirs a deep recognition in the amygdala that then signals our muscles to relax and our awareness to open. But the same is true of the Coastal Mugwort I find growing by the harbor, and the Cedar outside my bedroom window. Every landscape in the world contains aromatic plants whose scent shifts our consciousness toward connection with other than human realms. But there is a profound difference between what happens when I burn the needles of a Cedar I have stood beneath on sweltering summer afternoons and cold rainy winter nights, and what happens when I burn White Sage that was commercially harvested, wrapped in plastic, and sent hundreds of miles north. There is a different kind of magic involved.

> Devil's Club will not be ready to join you in your work until you have made your own relationship. And then your magic will not resemble mine.

THE FIRE IS HERE

Relational Plant Magic

A teacher can pass on lore about a god, or share their own experiences with that god, but that teacher's student can only truly come to know that god on their own terms. The best the teacher can do is to make an introduction and provide counsel on the cultivation of the relationship with that deity.

What is true of gods is also true of plants.

Here in my own bioregion, Devil's Club grows. Coast Salish peoples have long engaged the plant in protection magic -- but, though their ritual and medical science and technology inform my understanding of the plant, I do not engage it using their cultural practices. I came to know Devil's Club on its own terms, and visit it regularly, bringing offerings and prayers, and harvesting it according to instructions the plant itself gave me.

I can tell you that Devil's Club grows where the forest has been disrupted by a clearcut or a landslide or a flood and protects rich soils and the wildflowers that grow in them because its spiky stalks prevent big creatures from blundering over them and its great leaves shade the ground. I can tell you that it is so hard to remove by hand that it stopped the northward expansion of the railroads in British Columbia. I can tell you its green buds tipped with purple throb with erotic power in spring. But you still will not know Devil's Club. And Devil's Club will not be ready to join you in your work until you have made your own relationship. And then your magic will not resemble mine.

Martin Buber wrote "One cannot in the nature of things expect a little tree that has been turned into a club to put forth leaves." In the same way, one cannot expect a magic that involves the commodification of plants, or the treatment of plants as mere objects, to help us stop the relentless violence of the culture that declared the world a collection of resources for human consumption. If we want to engage plants as allies in revolutionary magic, we need to approach them as living beings and build deep and intimate relationships -- just like we would with any other comrade in the struggle.

Sean Donahue

Sean Donahue is a highly neurodivergent wild forest creature living on unceded WSANEC territory on the southern tip of what colonial cartographers now call Vancouver Island. He is a priest in the Black-Heart Line of the Feri Tradition and a teacher at Pacific Rim College where he teaches western herbal energetics, phytochemistry, mental health therapeutics, and subversive approaches to resume writing. His writing frequently appears at Gods & Radicals, in Plant Healer Magazine, and on his own blog, Green Man Ramblings.

The Wood at the World's End

William A. Young & Hanne T. Fisker

The ghost of a forest haunts the hills of southern Scotland. Today, a vast tract of moorland extends from the shores of the Irish Sea in the west to the North Sea in the east, its rolling hills peppered with conifer plantations and the grouse-butts of the shooting estates. This bleak country is named the Southern Uplands. It's a wild and lonely place, but, for all of its emptiness, not a natural one; travel back just a few centuries in time and these hills would have been covered by forests of ancient oak, juniper and birch, an ocean of whispering green leaves that has now vanished into memory. It is the ghost of the trees that haunts the hills; the memory of the living things that once defined this landscape, and made it something sacred.

As late as the 16th century, a walker could leave the town of Selkirk in the border country, and travel for twenty miles without stepping once from beneath the shadow of the trees. Now, on that same ground, there is barely a native tree in evidence. It was the hunger of the textile trade that felled the forest; woven wool formed the mainstay of the regional economy, and it was only on grassy, treeless hills that herds of sheep could be sustained. Before the demands of commerce, the forests fell back; and with them went a piece of the soul of the landscape, an old and vital thing that had given to the people of the land a great deal, over the years…

During the earlier middle ages the woodlands here had been known as Ettrick Forest. The crown had held it as a royal hunting preserve, a reserved tract of wilderness immune from the depredations of agriculture. At its heart lay a loch, named for St. Mary, by the shores of which stood a now ruinous church that was once the destination for a great annual pilgrimage led by the queen of the land. Just what it was that made the place sacred is now forgotten; a circumstance all too common in this particular part of the world.

Further back still than the middle ages, the forest stretched further, and its sanctity yet deeper. In the time of the Dark Ages, when Christianity was first arriving in the land and the name of St. Mary had yet to replace that of older, other mothers, this region was a part of the realm of the Brythonic Celts of the north. Now remembered chiefly in Wales, the old histories and legends recall their country as 'Yr Hen Ogledd': 'The Old North'. They were the native tribes of this landscape; the people who are now its inhabitants are still largely their descendants, divided from one another into nations named after their eventual conquerors, the Scots and the English.

In the time of the Brython, the forest was called 'Coed Celyddon': a name meaning the 'Caledonian Forest'. To the more settled lands further south, it formed an archetypal wilderness; the first great stretch of wild land encountered beyond the Roman Wall that had, for centuries, marked the edge of civilisation. Legends congregated here in numbers; the druidic faith had made of forests holy places, setting up schools in the woods and seeking contact with the otherworld in the embrace of the wild. In later times, their descendants, the prophet-bards of the Brython known as 'awenyddion' continued parts of their traditions, travelling to wild mountains and remote places to seek out the power of inspiration. It was in remoteness, in loneliness, in places beyond conventional society that they found their windows into the otherworld. There is a legacy here of primordial shamanism; of vision-quests in extreme places where the wall between the worlds of the living and the dead grows thin. The very oldest forms of human spirituality lingered in that wood beyond the world's end, sheltered by the shadows of the trees.

THE FIRE IS HERE

Of all the many spirits that haunted that forest, there is one in particular that may be singled out as of special importance; one that has gone on to achieve a great measure of fame. There are very few people alive today who have not at least heard of the name of Merlin, the Wizard; fewer know that this character is based upon a prophet-bard of the Old North, named Myrddin, who dwelt in Coed Celyddon.

Myrddin rose to importance as the bard to a king named Gwenddoleu, a great ruler in the north who appears to have had little truck with the Christian religion. Gwenddoleu enjoyed many triumphs and grew very famous, but his reign was eventually to be ended at a great battle called Arfderydd around the end of the 6th century. On this battlefield a great many of Myrddin's relatives and friends were slain, along with the lord who had provided him a home. As their blood flowed over the cold ground, Myrddin's world fell apart. Overcome by grief, he abandoned the savagery of human society and retreated into the forests to the north, living as a wild man among the hills. He was struck with a form of madness named, in Welsh, 'wyllt'; in Old Irish, the same notion was termed 'geillt'. It was a madness that was to bring with it gifts, a connection with the otherworld that was to transform him from just another court-bard into a figure of huge import for all of the Brython. It is in shamanism, once again, that we can see the roots of this change; among such cultures the origin of the shaman's gift, of their ability to interact with the otherworld, is often traced to a trauma or near-death experience, some dramatic event that shook them out of their conventional mind and brought them close to the spirits. In the madness of Myrddin we can glimpse a Celtic recension of this ancient impulse.

The gifts the madness bestowed were many. Myrddin became a poet and a prophet, an awenydd of the highest order who achieved a huge degree of fame all over the island of Britain. Even after the fall of Yr Hen Ogledd, his prophecies were recounted in Scotland well into the Middle Ages, forming a vital component of the folklore of the north; in Wales, they are still referenced right up until today. Of his poems, four works attributed to him are preserved in *The Black Book of Carmarthen*, and three in *The Red Book of Hergest*. While it is likely some editing took place at the hands of later redactors, it is entirely possible that the core of these poems do, indeed, constitute his work; there remains in their lines enough of the pagan, bardic spirit for this to be credibly so.

The stories told of Myrddin, or 'Merlin' as he was to become, passed beyond the Celtic world and gained considerable popularity all across medieval Europe. These legends, in turn, were to help inspire the works of the Romantic movement and, later, the fantasy genre. In both MacPherson's Ossian and in Tolkien's Gandalf the ghost of Myrddin may be glimpsed, the original archetype of the wise old wizard upon whom the figures draw. The images these later characters conjure are, however, only a partial expression of the

A BEAUTIFUL RESISTANCE

real Myrddin of legend; echoes only of an original spirit that was far more complex, far more rooted in reality. From the ghost of the mad bard, the awenydd of the wild, there is much that may be learned, lessons that can impact upon our modern lives in a way that tales of a fictional spell-weaver never can.

It was in pursuit of this ghost and in search of his lessons that a friend, Hanne T. Fisker, and I went into the hills that were once Coed Celyddon in September of 2015. We wished to enter what remained of the wilderness, to seek out the places in which Myrddin had walked, and to try to recover a little of the energy that had inspired him. We wished to try and bring some of his madness back from the empty hills, to shake up the sanity of everyday life. Such was the project – and, in the end, it was to prove more of a success than I'd ever dreamed. What happened to us was this...

We had chosen to commence our journey at the Wall itself; moving from the symbolic edge of civilisation deeper and deeper into the memory of the forest. The Wall had signified the limits, once; and it was beyond the limits that we wished to go.

We camped the first night at Sycamore Gap; the spot made famous by the film Robin Hood, where the ruins of the Wall are over-shadowed by the arcing branches of a great sycamore tree. In the darkness we sat on the Roman stones, watching shadows flicker at the edge of our vision, dancing on the slopes and among the branches of the tree. The suggestions of ghosts played in the night.

We walked along the Wall for a couple of days, then headed north across the border. We made our way up to the town of Langholm, before following the valley of the River Esk northwards towards hills that were growing ever higher. An old hillfort and a new Buddhist monastery were among the places where we rested our heads; we heard the wind sigh in the heights of the pine trees, saw cobwebs glisten with dew in the morning. Wading across a river made warm by a hot, mid-day sun, we arrived at a pair of ancient stone circles where the sensations of place stirred us in a fashion wonderful and strange. In a grove decked out with statues and coloured cloths, we discovered a reincarnation of a holy place from the druidic past; breathed in the old with the scent of pine needles, and fell back into it in a fashion most wonderful to *feel*. From the intellectual bones of the project, the flesh of feeling began to grow; maps and lists of stories became entangled with living, potent experiences, with memories of scent and sight and touch. Fed upon such an elixir, the ghosts began to come alive...

And then, we walked over the hills to Carrifran.

We'd walked in sunlight over a ridge, to see a broad, steep-edged valley spread out before us. As we stood on the hillside, the warmth of the sunlight gently touched our skin, while the wind caressed it, and brought to us a scent

THE FIRE IS HERE

of the heather blossom that rose thickly from the purple-clad hills of the declining summer. There was a sense of warmth, and peace, and freedom. Following the track a little way down the hill, we found a spot where a knoll on the hillside provided a perfect viewpoint over the valley below. Sitting in its centre, there lay an ancient standing stone. We paused beside it, to take in the view.

Before us, a number of steep-sided hills rose up from the floor of the valley. Between them were sharp little glens, miniature sub-valleys carved out by the ice millennia ago. Most were bare, empty; but in one, however, something a little different could be glimpsed. A haze of green obscured the hillside, a soft, thick mass of vegetation little in evidence anywhere else. What we were seeing was the early stages of the growth of a forest; young trees just over a decade old slowly reclaiming their place upon the hillside. We were gazing down upon the rebirth of the forest, upon a place called the Carrifran Wildwood.

The project at Carrifran began in the year 2000. It is the undertaking of an organisation called the Borders Forest Trust, supported by the larger and better-known John Muir Trust. The purpose of their work is to restore a little part of the old native forest of southern Scotland, bringing back to one little valley the full collection of native species that once made their home there. Fifteen years after its inception, the forest is growing up nicely; the trees are growing tall, and wildlife is thriving. It is quite a place to see, these days.

From our hillside viewpoint we at length descended, crossing the first valley and, by the evening, walking into Carrifran. We camped there, by a little river that runs through it, on ground strewn with patches of wild flowers bright as jewels scattered over the earth.

When morning came, we woke to the rushing of the stream. Insects buzzed through the air, and the faint patter of drizzle stroked the surface of the tent. We packed up our little dwelling place, and walked upstream, following a path that ran upwards and inwards, entering deeper and deeper into the woods.

The scent of wet leaves filled the air; the atmosphere thick with organicity. Verdant greenery wrapped itself around the path, plants of the forest floor grown to shoulder height at this late stage of the summer, fencing us into a swaying, breathing corridor of life. The shining shapes of insects crawled over their surfaces, navigating their way between droplets of gleaming water that studded the surface of the leaves. Above, the trees rose; a variegated mosaic of leaves of a diversity and a richness vastly different to the dull, serried rows of plantation pine that cover so much of Scotland. Their green tide flooded up the hillsides, only at great length fading out in the higher reaches, far above us, to be replaced by the blazing purple of blooming heather and the starker grey of screes.

As we moved on, the rain began to thicken. Droplets thudded onto leaves, spattering against our hoods

THE FIRE IS HERE

and beating out a staccato song that filled the forest. A veil of clouds descended to wreath the hilltops, stoking the waterfalls and enlivening the air with whirling mist. The outer world was soon shut off, and we vanished into a vibrant, natural inner world that seemed to capture perfectly the memory of the forest past.

Quite a picture it is, that has been painted on this valley in shades of green, a picture of glories past and future yet to come. Held within its embrace, amidst the scents and sensations of that wild old world, we began to feel transported. The imagery and the evocations connected so very well with the legends in which we had been steeping ourselves for days, that the latter began to be called forth of their own accord. Stories came to life, in a most unexpected way.

Within the heart of the woods there sits a little stone building; half bothy, half shed, kitted out with benches upon which to sit, and with stacks of the materials made use of by the planters. Its roof is of turf, its walls are of drystone, riddled with gaps that admit narrow cracks of light into the interior darkness. We intended to pause there for a brief spell only, to make use of the shelter to cook up some food, out of the way of the strengthening rain. However, as we finished our meal and our coffee, something else entirely began to happen.

There is something in the presence of darkness that frees up the mind. The absence of images calls forth images; the rituals of shamans past were performed in the dark of the night, where they danced or chanted for hours into exhaustion, so that the lack of energy would shut down the barriers of the mind and permit the world held chained within to escape. Once free, it would paint whatever pictures it willed on the blank canvas of the darkness; summoning up images from the recesses of the consciousness to play over the surface of the blank black screen.

We'd been walking for days, by this point, over hill and valley. Our minds had fallen deep into the dreamworld of mythic imagery, and, now, called up perhaps by the tiredness of the journey and the darkness of that little, womb-like chamber, something of that dreamworld began to come forth.

We stopped journeying, and paused instead to listen. Ceasing to seek, we instead opened up, letting the world around us come pouring in, permitting impressions to arise in whatever way they chose to.

Gentle hands touched gentle hands, and the senses sprang to life. Once heightened, awareness extended outwards, creeping along the channels of hearing into the space outwith the walls. It stepped into the wind as that river of air embraced the stones and whipped its way by. In my mind's eye, an image of ravens fluttering in that wind took hold and, as it did so, I was engulfed with the sense that something in the air had spun and turned and focused in – and was looking *back*, right at me.

Words flowed, and images after them. A torrent of creation, springing up from who knows where and sending out an urgent, quiet flow of rhythmic syllables into the close darkness. Spinning, circling words that depicted and sound-tracked the sensations of the place, at once a response to it and a part of carrying it further; a shaman's chant that came to fill that secret little world and take us deeper and deeper in.

When I emerged back into the daylight, out of that old darkness and into a semblance of clarity once again, something had changed. There was a knot untied, a chain cast off; something was freed, and it has been running ever since, slowly growing stronger. Where the words and the footsteps they guide will lead I do not yet know, but I am happy to see where they will carry me, and to move on with the journey. What it was that happened I in all honesty do not know; I cannot say with any certainty, based on my own experience, whether I was being swept up into a world of my own mind's creation, or one that exists in some kind of elsewhere, touched for a moment in the dark. It may have been magic; it may have been mental. It may have been either, or neither, or something else altogether; and it is this next thing that I will tell you that touches the heart of the matter.

It does not matter.

Let me tell you why...

The experience I had in that little hut, and so many other experiences like it I've encountered over the course of the years, have been among the most intense that I have ever experienced. They have been

wonderful; ecstatic, pleasurable, fascinating, meaningful. Even if the sensations, images and ideas that have flowed through me have been illusions conjured up by my own mind, the actual, living moment of being in their grip has felt far more real, more vital, than 'reality' ever has. Illusion overpowers the dull grey of normality, and spins the stuff of dream around your steps.

There is a beast that chews upon this world, consuming it slowly. Every reader of this journal knows its varied names: capitalism, greed, the machine age. The compulsive consumption of luxuries required by our modern economic system is swiftly stripping the world of life. This process is underpinned by a sacred consumerist truth: that it is possessing these luxuries that will make us happier. That self-interest lies in preserving the material interest; that consumer goods are good for consumers.

Against this, from out of the darkness in the heart of the forest a counter-logic arises; that happiness comes from intensity of experience. That adventure, emotion, explosions of sensation and breath-taking flights of vision are innately better than – for example – a microwave oven; and that the most effective route to finding such experiences lies within us, not without. There was no spending at all required to conjure up that powerful energy that throbbed through the darkness under Carrifran's crags; simply immersion of our minds in myth, a stillness, a darkness, and the willingness to explore it. Such things are found far easier in the silence of the wild places than amidst the endless distractions of the city; it is in retreat into the wilderness that we can most easily find that which holds real meaning, that which can, quite possibly, undercut the basis of the consumer culture and provide one of the building blocks of a better world.

We return to Myrddin. Just to the west of Carrifran, past the high cliff called Raven Crag, there rises a hill called Hart Fell. This mountain was named after the prophet; after a legend that he transformed into a deer to flee from his enemies, and ran across its slopes in that lithe, animal form. He roamed far and wide among these mountains; but somewhere among them was one particular place that is described in the poems, that formed more of a home for him than most. It was a glade at a hilltop, where a spring arose and an apple tree stood. Here, in his glade, Myrddin sat in his madness, lamenting his losses – and cherishing his gains.

He had nothing. The descriptions that remain to us show him as a mostly naked, unwashed, hairy thing of the forest, more beast than man, filling onlookers with alarm. He was, in modern terms, the lowest of the low, a homeless, worthless vagrant contributing nothing to society. And yet... it is he, more than any other figure of that time, who has, inarguably, left the greatest legacy upon the world. It is he who is remembered best; he who is the keeper of magic, the window to the otherworld, the archetype of enchantment.

The notion of Myrddin is an inversion of reason; the voice of a sacred madness that sits in the wilderness, laughing at the frivolous constructions piled up behind the Wall. To seek out the lesson that silent voice is speaking nothing is necessary but this; to journey into the wild, and to open up to what will come to you. This was the ancient practice of all of our ancestors, in the time of the hunter-gatherers; the first religion, the inevitable consequence of our original life in the wild. It may not be magic, but in fact something far greater; the force that dwells in the blood and the bone, that enables us to make something out of nothing, to find satisfaction not in things, but in simply living our lives. The inevitable consequence of dwelling for millions of years in the wild with nothing is the ability to find the most profound satisfaction in the wild, with nothing. That this remains to us is not magic, but the simple science of evolution; that our nature, formed in nature, we can return to in stepping back into nature. It raises the possibility that the destructive tendencies of our modern culture may be curbed not through revolutionary violence, but simply through convincing people to depart from it, in the free pursuit of a better, happier life.

In the wood at the world's end, the ghost of a forest is returning to life. In Carrifran Wildwood the shoots are rising up; the shadow of the leaves hangs once again over the earth. It is a nucleus, a seed alone; but the branches are spreading. Feed it, and it will grow strong; nurture it, and it will nourish you in return. As Celyddon rises again, so too may its spirits; and another world may be re-awoken, within this one. To visit it is no great hardship.

William A. Young & Hanne T. Fisker

William is a Scottish writer, based in Edinburgh. He spends far too much time roaming around in the wilder portions of northern Europe chasing spirits. Hanne is a photographer from Denmark, now based in the wild west of Ireland, with a passion for the magical and the mystical.

THE FIRE IS HERE

Myrddin's Scribe

Lorna Smithers

We hold the inner space for God above:
clear, calm, silent, only to hear *him* galloping
in like a forest: thunder of deer-storm,
cacophony of boar-grunt bristled as pine.
Naked and skinny he takes his throne:
a steep stone beside Molendinar Burn.

Though he lives off only common air,
his words are juicy berries,
succulent apples, cracking hazelnuts
whose wisdom only chewing can divine.
Some have horns and antlers. Some are stags
alive with rude desire. Some have swinging udders.
Some have feathers and fluttering heart-beats
racing between sky and heaven.

My heart stutters and leaps when Kentigern
commands me to take quill and vellum,
with a shaking, itinerant hand pen
huge, outrageous monsters
taking me on shaggy backs
with clip-clop of trotters to dance goat-foot
in a glade or suckle swine. An old boar
runs at me with curved tusks.
Suddenly I'm helpless; lying bleeding, gored,

on the forest floor as fur-coated warriors
step forward with stumps of spears,
twisted shields, jagged swords.
Each bears a death story:
a severed limb, broken head, belly gouged.
They do not stop arriving from Celyddon's darkness

in charred pieces ranting about fiery skies,
falling through everlasting night,
white-light, lightning soldiers,
filling my head with catastrophic pain
and unending war until I scream: "no more!"

I want to turn back to the forest. Run back
to the wild creatures but see we've gone too far
unless some prophecy can stop it.
I dip my quill in the ink,
pen these roaring and bloody words
coursing through my veins marking stiff spears
and gaping wounds. A mad man's angst soothed only
by sketches of leafy foliage, the smile
of a dog, the face of a bear.

My last life seeps into the vellum,
snatched away by Kentigern.
Disliking what he sees,
he throws it into Molendinar Burn.

In my dark cell I die slowly,
taking hope in Myrddin's words:
his prophecies will be inscribed again
in a sea-town of the Cymry. Fierce animal
portraits and green branching letters
will be inscribed again and again,
until we learn to love the forest
and turn from war.

Lorna Smithers

Lorna Smithers is an awenydd, Brythonic polytheist and devotee of Gwyn ap Nudd based in Lancashire. She believes to change the world we must renew our myths. She is the author of Enchanting the Shadowlands *and blogs at* Signposts in the Mist. *She is also a contributor to* Awen ac Awenydd, Dun Brython, *and* Gods & Radicals.

Wonder is a weapon, too
Gordon MacLellan

Wonder leads to enquiry, enquiry leads to knowledge
—Thomas Aquinas

I create celebrations. With infants in nurseries, classes in primary schools, clumps of teenagers, families in parks, retired people in slightly stuffy rooms, just about anyone really, and just about anywhere. As "Creeping Toad", I am an artist and storyteller, finding ways of helping people explore their relationship with the world around them.

This can be quite spectacular. There have been processions of giant tree people, sets of toadstools with associated songs, 60 children reciting poems inspired by *Gawain and the Green Knight* in the ruins of an old hall, lanterns reflecting in still water. But in conversation with the dynamic and revolutionary, or even simply ardent, campaigners, "educational work" sounds tame and not very exciting and (when I'm feeling particularly paranoid) easily dismissed.

A BEAUTIFUL RESISTANCE

I believe, however, that "we live in a world worthy of celebration[16]" and without the sense of celebration I'm not sure what else will follow. We often do not live in a way that respects celebration but developing an awareness of wonder might be one of the steps to changing attitudes and actions. The processes that draw people into a relationship with their world are essentially simple. *Listen.* Listen to your senses, to the birds, to the wind that blows and the grass that grows and what you can't hear, *watch,* and what you can't watch *touch, smell, taste* maybe. And then reflect and feel and play and hopefully out of that comes a sense of value and worth and joy.

The Thomas Aquinas quote feels very apt. My work draws on wonder and encourages enquiry and the discovery of knowledge: finding things out, hopefully by experience and hopefully for yourself. Creeping Toad projects invite investigation and challenge. The essence it seems to me (not always the practice) of good education is to encourage independent thought - to provoke those senses of wonder and enquiry and discovery. Education should encourage change as new people explore ideas and find answers for themselves. Maybe that's why dictatorial regimes suppress free education and why more subtle systems do their best to control and restrict it: good education encourages a sense of personal worth and an understanding of what is going on around us. I try not to be too cynical and to hope.

And for me, my gentle, laughing work in environmental discovery and community growth slides into that "in hope of revolution" section on the pie-chart of society. This isn't work that foments unrest and shakes the castles of power. This work is about inviting people to wonder. To pause and realise that the world we all live in is wonderful and that it's worth fighting for. In gentle storywalks, in rambling explorations, in creating community celebrations of local parks, in finding the stories of the giants who hide among the trees, we find that we can work together and that as individuals and groups and communities we can laugh and work and celebrate together. That's what I do. And then I hope that somehow, somewhere, somewhen, it might add strength to a wind of change. Sometimes, this can all sound so sweet and twee but here also are the smile on the skull, the cold sigh of extinction and fossilisation, the egg that never hatches, the tadpoles who feed just about everyone else in their pond.

I'm an animist. A shaman listening to the people I work with and listening to the places we work in, finding strategies to let the two experience each other. That animism has run with me most of my life - some of the spirits I associate with have run with me just as long. It is a fierce passion that keeps me on my feet and working when it looks like we'll never make a difference. The long, slow lifetimes of trees and the even longer and slower ones of mountains remind me to accept other timescales for change and evolution. There are gods who watch and comment and nudge me gently (or give me a hefty shove). There is laughter and silence and power in the night that leaves me trembling and flooded with moonlight.

And for most of "my" people all this is not there. The pagan side of me is me and mine: it informs Boggart-water.jpegand inspires my work but for most of the groups I work with it is irrelevant. They book me because I deliver a high quality professional process that does not presume to judge, convert (corrupt?), or preach. For myself, it is important that I act as a creative technician - a storyteller who gets imaginations and senses working, but the interpretation of what we find and develop belongs to the participants in a process. It is not my place to tell people what to believe.

And I do not meet an Earth that wants people to believe in *this* or in *that* or even in *the next thing*. All I hear from "my" gods is that they are looking for an Earth that is loved - probably in as many different

16 Quote from my book "Celebrating Nature", published by Capall Bann a manual for community celebrations

THE FIRE IS HERE

ways as there are people. They do not want converts or worship. They hope for a world that is growing strong and loving people - whether those people are human, animal, plant or mineral, in flesh or out of flesh.

I am a storyteller, I spin wonder with words, experiences and joy. I live in a world worthy of celebration and that will be my contribution to any change that shakes the human world into a more harmonious shape.

"If I can't dance, I don't want to be part of your revolution" Emma Goldman

GORDON MACLELLAN

Gordon MacLellan is an environmental artist and storyteller. Better known as Creeping Toad he works with groups to explore ways of celebrating the relationships between people, places and wildlife. In Pagan communities, he is called Gordon the Toad and has spent 25 years talking, writing, inspiring and irritating people, breaking rules with laughter and enjoying himself a lot.

Of Worlding:
Stories of Becoming and Social Hope

Kadmus

"I tell of bodies changed to other forms;
You Gods, who have changed even this tale,
Inspire my enterprise and lead my lay
In one continuous song…"
Ovid's *Metamorphoses*

"The first of the goddesses said to me…
We know how to speak many false things as if they were true;
And when we will, to utter the truth."
Hesiod *Theogony* 24, 27-28

"…if you tell stories in the summertime when the crops are growing, the corn, beans, squash, etc. may stop to listen to you and forget their duties – to grow and produce. It is believed that stories are so powerful that things in nature will listen to them and get confused, and forget what it is that they are supposed to do."
Hitakonanu'Laxk
The Grandfathers Speak: Native American Folk Tales of the Lenape People

The pagan life was lived in and through stories. This is both a statement of historical necessity (old cultures told stories because they couldn't write them down and they told them when and how they did precisely because they needed to be preserved through performance) and a fact constitutive of paganism itself (keeping wisdom alive only in and through repetition of it in narrative and song effects the type of wisdom preserved and pursued, as well as the manner in which we can think at all). We can, and should, of course derive from pagan ways of life, as well as their stories and wisdom-teachings, insights that fit the demands of political, metaphysical, and theological inquiry. This is frequently what I have tried to do in my work; but we should also recognize that often it is from the story structure itself, the sheer fact and nature of pagan stories, that some of the chiefest metaphysical lessons can be drawn.

To say that pagan cultures are story cultures is to say that they were all in essence oral cultures. They each were born before writing and even those that later developed writing remained oral in nature if not in technical fact. Philosophy and Science came from the birth of new poetries under the influences of writing. Consider the epic poem turned high metaphysics of Parmenides and the proto-scientific stanzas of Empedocles; these new poetic forms arose from a struggle to understand and master new cognitive capabilities provided by writing itself. We witness the same thing in Plato's transformation of orality into literality through the invention of the philosophical dialogue. Writing allowed us to do things and think things we never could before[17], and led us to forget things we once knew clearly. It gave rise to an increasing obsession with certainty and control, and a decreased appreciation for the inevitability of change.

As Socrates himself feared, writing is both a cure and a poison. The thinking of oral cultures is inherent-

17 For a robust defense of this view as it applies to the development of conceptual thought in Ancient Greece see Erik Havlock's Preface to Plato as well as his paper "The Linguistic Task of the Presocratics" and Kevin Robb's "Preliterate Ages and the Linguistic Art of Heraclitus" both in *Language and Thought in Early Greek Philosophy* Kevin Robb ed.

ly contextual and aggregative. As Bruno Snell once put it in regards to the original oral nature of Homer, "Of course the Homeric man had a body exactly like that of the later Greeks, but he did not know it qua body, but merely as the sum total of his limbs."[18] Such insights led the philosopher Paul Feyerabend to claim that oral cultures saw the world as made up of aggregates without essences or grounding substance.[19] In fact we can push this further and claim that oral cultures are essentially tied to an Event Ontology in which events, contexts, and relations but not objects and things are real. This means that such cultures saw the world as an aggregate of changes, events of becoming, and not as a structure of objects in lawful interaction. Abstract concepts are all but impossible to formulate or contemplate in a culture used to poetic recitation as the model of privileged speech. While this seems like a dramatic claim, when you try to get even heavily literate contemporary people to consider the nature of justice in general, rather than specific concrete examples of justice, or beauty in general rather than given instantiations, there is a clear cognitive struggle. I witness it in my students every day. What is a struggle for us was all but an impossibility for oral cultures, especially since inquiry into general abstract concepts is unlikely to even arise in such a culture.

The reason I have stressed this frequently overlooked and under-appreciated point about history is that the manner in which old pagan cultures told stories is one with the way in which they saw the world and thought about it. Now, it is not at all my point that somehow literate cultures are superior to illiterate ones. In fact the point I have in mind is rather the reverse. There is, of course, an amazing power in writing and the abstract thought and argumentation it gives us access to, but in adding one power you often enough destroy another. To put this more bluntly, history is a story of change and not necessarily progress and it is clear to most of us that there were truths and abilities our pagan ancestors had that we have largely lost and seek to regain.

There is a Lenape story about how the sugar maple came to have sweet sap. Here is a variation on the story:

The Lenape had been trading with their southern neighbors and were jealous of the rich sugar they always had to eat and trade, but sugar cane didn't grow in Lenape land. Worse than this, however, the southern people were prone to wars amongst themselves and visiting them to obtain sugar was dangerous. So the people turned to their good friend, the spirit Nanapush, and asked for sugar of their own. Now Nanapush was very clever but he was also cautious. The people valued sugar now, he worried, but sugar cane could give sugar up very easily and if he coaxed it to grow in the north the people would no longer appreciate sugar as they now did. He was pondering the problem when, one day, a group of hungry wendigos decided to follow him to his hidden home in the mountains so that they could attack and eat him. Nanapush arrived at his home unaware that he was being stalked by the dangerous spirit-beasts. But Nanapush's house was surrounded by maple trees to which he had always been kind, and seeing the wendigos gathering in the distance and realizing that Nanapush was in trouble, the trees immediately changed their leaves to bright reds and yellows. When the wendigos came upon the home it looked as if it was surrounded with a wall of wild fire. Terrified, the monsters fled and never returned. At that moment Nanapush realized what had happened and that he could both give the trees a gift in return for their rescue and give the Lenape what they wanted. He turned the sap of the trees sweet and taught the Lenape both to cherish the maple, which must be tall and healthy to produce rich sap, and how to perform the work involved in turning the sap to

> history is a story of change and not necessarily progress.

---

18   *Homer's Iliad: Modern Critical Interpretations* Harold Bloom ed. p. 51
19   See "Reason, Xenophanes and the Homeric Gods" in Feyerabend's *Farewell to Reason*

A BEAUTIFUL RESISTANCE

sugar. In this way the Lenape were able to get sugar only through both the respect and care they showed the trees especially when tapping them and through the hard work involved in boiling the sap.

This is a story of change. It is not a story of how the gods created the maple tree, but rather a tale of how together the actions of humanity, the trees, and the gods brought about a change in the world. As Ovid says, it is a tale of "bodies changed to other forms". Although some pagan cultures do indeed have tales of ultimate creation, it is usually not too hard to demonstrate that these are later tales built on an older substructure of what we might call tales of change. Tales of ultimate beginnings, like prophecies of ultimate ends such as stories of the Norse Ragnarok, attempt to create expansive narratives in which the rest of the world's events fit. These attempt to be stories of order, which set each thing in its place. They are often also wrapped up in political projects of establishing rulership and enforcing various deified human leaders. Tales of change, on the other hand, happen almost inevitably *en media res*. They take us to a setting already established with stories already underway. The Lenape already know Nanapush, the wendigos already hate him, the people to the south already trade sugar and engage in war, and so on. My claim is that the pagan worldview, largely because of its vital oral roots, is always of a world *en media res* even when later stories like the *Theodicy* of Hesiod or tales of the Norse Ragnarok attempt to push against this.

Ancient epics don't start in the middle of the story for no reason, and it is not that we have just lost the other pieces (although often many pieces have indeed been lost). For oral poets, or rather oral performers of the poetry that would have been passed down from generation to generation for hundreds of years, with slight additions along the way, slowly building a mighty narrative treasury, there is no beginning nor end to the tales. What I previously called the aggregate nature of the worldview can also be called an additive nature that follows the logic of "and also". There is always another tale to follow and another tale that preceded. We see this very clearly in the traditional ending that appears throughout the Homeric Hymns where the poet closes by stating to the goddess or god "and now I will remember you and another song also." There is always "another song also".

We see the inescapable additive nature even in the great tales of ends and beginnings. Hesiod's *Theogony* may tell the tale of the gods reproducing the world into existence but there is no ultimate explanation, aside from the existence of sheer desire, for any of the process, and ultimately the first goddess, Gaia, is uncreated. This open-ended aspect is even stronger when we contemplate the ultimate "order" that the *Theogony* achieves. It is clear, both in Hesiod and throughout Greek myth and culture, that Zeus' rule is a political compromise and an exceptionally fragile one at that. It is frequently hinted that his rule will eventually end, as did that of his father and grandfather, and a new order begin. The "and then" continues with no order or meaning being assured absolutely. We see this same point in the specter of "fate" which it is clear the gods themselves cannot escape, though it is always unclear why. Zeus is as bound by fate as Odin, despite the work the latter puts into avoiding the fall of the gods. In this sense it can be argued that fate for the ancient pagans meant more the inevitability of change, even and especially for the gods, than a predetermined end. The beginning and end of Norse mythology shares these aspects with the Greek. The beginning is not really a beginning, for we are left to wonder about more absolute foundations and explanations for the existence of the giant Ymir, out of whose death the world is formed, whilst the fall of the gods in Ragnarok clearly points to a new beginning and a new story. What is fated is change, is becoming.

Strictly speaking, the foundational texts of most of the world's monotheistic religions are no different. The Bible derives from oral traditions and is, like Homer, the outcome of a complex process of writing and editing an already very ancient and complicated oral corpus. The beginnings and endings are similarly imperfect, open-ended, and incomplete. It is with this thought that I would like to proffer a rather tricky idea. I have often used the term "pagan" for cultures that might not seem to obviously fit my own understanding of the term. I think a pagan culture is one with a multiplicity of divine forces irreducible to one ultimate one. In this piece, however, I have discussed one Native American culture that often posits a singular Great Spirit. I have often elsewhere also discussed traditional African cultures such as that of the Akan people, which sometimes also posits a singular ultimate creator god.

Despite appearances I am not exactly as confused or inconsistent as I might seem, or at the very least I have some hope that this is not the case. At the most basic level a culture can be officially monotheist in religion without being monotheist in metaphysics or theology. The reverse is also possible; Plato, for example, was officially polytheist and many have taken Neoplatonism to similarly be polytheist, but I would argue it is metaphysically monotheist. The diversity of divine things are reducible to one ultimate divine principle in Plato and Platonism and this principle is unchanging and transcendental. This is the very heart of monotheism, the claim that there is some one unchanging thing that orders and structures all. It is, as you can see, an abstract position inaccessible, I would argue, to an oral culture that has not been seduced by the power of words to turn events and experiences into abstract objects. This is why what I consider pagan cultures tend to see even their idea of the One Great God, if they have one, as some form of community or political leader, even if a very distant one, rather than a metaphysic principle from which each thing takes its being and by which it is maintained.

> There is always "another song also"

In any culture then, in any time, the stories of change and becoming – when they are truly about becoming and not simply about pre-ordained structure playing itself inevitably out – are always pagan in their own right. Stories of change, perspectives *en media res*, are always the enemies of established order - which brings me, in fact, to my overall concern in this essay. Political action, indeed all social and communal action, requires both the hope for, and threat of, change. It is a monotheist strain in culture and thought, whether or not that culture and thought even admits the existence of any god, that assumes things are set as they are or that change cannot happen. There is so much that paganism and polytheism can offer our deeply ailing world, but high in the list of things is a social hope that stretches from the immediate possibility of change in our present lives to the hope born of the inevitability of global and cosmic change. The pagan world is woven of the stories of becoming. Gods and people, animals and plants, worlds and voids and giants and dragons - all become. We might say that fate is the worlding of the world, the drive and inevitable fact of coming-to-be and passing-away, which assures us that we must work to *world*, to become, in a direction that will be better than that from which we seek to escape. But the assumption that the battles we would fight are hopeless, that the chains beneath which our world strains are unbreakable, that is the ghost of a monotheism that would reassure itself that the world is as it should be and that cosmic force has placed the whip in the hands of the master or the money in the vault of the bank. To this prospect the stories of becoming respond, *"all masters fall eventually."*

Kadmus

Kadmus is a practicing ceremonial magician with a long standing relationship to the ancient Celtic deities. His interests and practice are highly eclectic but a deep commitment to paganism is the bedrock upon which they all rest. Kadmus is also a published academic with a Ph.D. in philosophy teaching at the college level.

Scrolls

Catriona McDonald

I.
Trailing stiff fingers across seeping sandstone,
deeper and deeper into the thrumming earth.
Beneath the sacred hill, down, down, down, plunging
in spiral darkness.

Empty corridors shining with fae fire,
Slipping faster, flowing emptiness surrounds
times before, drifting ghosts across root and rock
show clear memory.

II.
Learning more, travel's harder, words choking.
Reading, absorbing, mind getting cotton-stuffed,
mental obesity, over-indulgence
in academic bloat.

Right action traded for righteous sloth slowly
blocks the tor-tunnels. Bookcases line Gwynn's halls,
scroll after scroll, book after tome, dust choking
between deadened leaves.

Shove, shred effortlessly-accumulated
avalanches, begging for clarity.
Trade gifts of intuition for book-knowledge,
pay a heavy price.

III.
Ash-bright fingers brush mine, pull me free with a
rustling pop. *Why do you children rive and slay*

experience for stacks of plied symbols? Blackened
eyes crease, not unkind.

Seek the heart-songs, sing them strong.
Dance the dreaming, trailing magic in your wake.
Hold close the fire until it burns your mind
to ash and dust motes,

purging hollow wisdom for brighter knowledge.
Forsake the deadly seduction of cyphers.
Sever, sunder, wrack, rend, tear without mercy
lies clutched too long.

Wild Truth-shaper, rise! Brand the blood of your tribe
in memory's dance, knotting wyrd as you will.
Flight born of anguish, but so sweet is its draught.
Hunt with me and soar.

Catriona McDonald

Catriona McDonald is an Ovate Grade member of the Order of Bards, Ovates & Druids, and a proud denizen of the Assabet River bioregion of central Massachusetts. Further Druidic ramblings can be found on her blog, The Druid's Well, at http://thedruidswell.com.

Footsteps in the Embers

THE SUI GENERIS SERMON

Dr Bones

Sui Generis: (Latin): a phrase meaning "of its (his, her, or their) own kind; in a class by itself; unique"

Brothers and Sisters, we hold a new century in our hands yet our ideas are still waiting to catch up! Our heads are not only haunted, they are home to creatures of another age!

Everywhere dinosaurs walk amongst us, their slow marching steps matching the reluctant chugging along of the thoughts in their head. There is no need to find John Hammond to play god! No no! No need for expensive labs to resurrect the eggs of forgotten ideology. They are here, friends, HERE, these twisted children afraid to venture out of the nest!

They are easiest to spot amongst the Right: folks beholden to "better times" wishing to "make America great again." The fact that the "prosperity" and "greatness" was the result of a titanic war against global superpowers leaving the US alone as THE global manufacturer is often overlooked[20], as is the glaring and stark fact that this prosperity was not shared by everyone. Even in the sunniest, happiest days of our Empire trees in the South still bore strange fruit. Still, the time-lust throbs deeply for ancient days among these people, and they hold up crumbling documents now mostly ignored as a solution to everything. "This isn't what the founding fathers wanted! We need to get back to our principles!" And principles INDEED! A democracy for white landowners, chattel slavery for people of color, and outright genocide for the Natives! I cannot forget that it was under the American Flag that the historic Black Fort of Florida[21] was attacked, a shining beacon of hope and freedom manned by hundreds of runaway slaves; a burgeoning culture wiped out for fear it would inspire others to understand that they could manage their own affairs without a state, without a "master." That famous cry "Give me liberty or give me death" didn't only belong to Patrick Henry! It was the motto of the fort's defenders, and its battle cry AGAINST American troops is conspicuously ABSENT in the history books.

Just as well they gloss over the strikers killed, the immigrants kept in line by the policeman's club, the outlawing of entire languages, and the planned destruction of cultures that took thousands of years to create. For all this my heart is to be *moved*? I am to believe all these are aberrations spanning hundreds of years, that if only we got back to what the "founders wanted" all of this would have *never happened*? It matters little what they "wanted," this is what they DID. Jefferson wrote like an Anarchist but ruled like a king. The case is closed: all of American history stands as evidence to the true nature of the "FREEDOM" we enjoy, evidence we're still producing every day as we continue to export it to Iraq, Afghanistan, Libya, Ukraine, and Syria.

But, while the dinosaurs of the right still lurch and roar into the air so too do other strange creatures: human mega-fauna of an ideological Ice Age. Here stands the tottering behemoth of the Left chewing on the living grass of authentic social movements and the bones of failed revolutions. Amongst them you'll find the protest warriors and their signs, the ageing "scientists" of Marxist-Leninism, and the playful petit students

---

20   http://www.zerohedge.com/news/20140328/goldenera1950s60swasanomalynotdefaultsetting
21   https://libcom.org/history/negrofortmassacre

A BEAUTIFUL RESISTANCE

who rally for revolution until they're promised free tuition. Most dangerous of all is the run-of-the-mill liberal, a shifty species who is "10 degrees to the Left of center in good times, 5 degrees to the Right of center when it affects them personally."[22] Within all these venerable beasts you find living fossils of practice and ideology: "We need to let the people in power know we aren't happy with this! Let's stage a protest!"; "We need a vanguard party to educate the masses. Once they are under our command we'll take state power!"; "If we just pick the right candidate in the primary and get them elected, we can fix this whole mess!" Time and time again age old solutions to problems that have morphed beyond recognition are trotted out, and time and time again they are countered because they've simply become predictable.

Are the ideologies of these dinosaurs and mega-fauna worth saving?

Shared between them is the subjugation of the individual to a collective desire or ideal: To the Patriots (and the Democrats) I am only so good as long as I am a good citizen. And what then is that? Stirner, champion of the Individual, regards it thus:

"One must give up *himself*, and live only for the State. One must act "disinterestedly," not want to benefit *himself*, but the State. Hereby the latter has become the true person before whom the individual personality vanishes; not I live, but it lives in me. Therefore, in comparison with the former self-seeking, this was unselfishness and *impersonality* itself. Before this god — State — all egoism vanished, and before it all were equal; they were without any other distinction..."

"...it is not the "born" who is free, nor yet I who am free either, but the "deserving" man, the honest *servant* (of his king; of the State; of the people in constitutional States). Through *service* one acquires freedom, *i.e.* acquires "deserts," even if one served — mammon. One must deserve well of the State, i.e. of the principle of the State, of its moral spirit. He who *serves* this spirit of the State is a good citizen..."[23]

I exist not so much as a unique individual but as an American citizen or "patriot." However much I digress from this symbol I am to identify with (Christian, Pro-Military, Pro-War, Pro-Bernie Sanders, Capitalist) I lose value in the eyes of the State. A cursory view of how radicals and people of color are treated by the police vs. the very wealthy or very white should supply enough evidence of this. Since following the commands of the State makes me deserving of identity, to rebel or follow my own path results in the forfeiture of my humanity. Since I am no longer human I am treated not as a person but as a thing. I am a "vagabond," a "homeless," an "animal," a "criminal," a "thug," a "militant," a "communist," a "terrorist,"

> To the Patriots (and the Democrats) I am only so good as long as I am a good citizen... But the dreamers of the Left would brook me no freedom either, for to them I am not a unique individual, I am a laborer, a "worker,"

22   Phil Ochs, "Love me, I'm a Liberal" https://www.youtube.com/watch?v=u52Oz54VYw

23   Max Stirner, *The Ego and His Own*, pg 91 and 95

A BEAUTIFUL RESISTANCE

and as such I can be beaten, imprisoned, tortured or killed at leisure.

Have we not seen this with *our own eyes*?!?

But the dreamers of the Left would brook me no freedom either, for to them I am not a unique individual, I am a laborer, a "worker," and so:

"...labor is our sole value all the same: that we are *laborers* is the best thing about us, this is our significance in the world, and therefore it must be our consideration too and must come to receive *consideration*. What can you meet us with? Surely nothing but — labor too. Only for labor or services do we owe you a recompense, not for your bare existence; not for what you are *for yourselves* either, but only for what you are *for us*."[24]

I become merely the value I produce, the task I supply for society. Stirner is careful to note that labor need not be enslaving if "on the contrary, when everyone is to cultivate himself into man (i.e. a true, unique individual)...every labor is to have the intent that the man be satisfied."[25] But this is not the labor we undertake today:

"condemning a man to *machine-like labor* amounts to the same thing as slavery. If a factory worker must tire himself to death twelve hours and more, he is cut off from becoming man... He who in a pin factory only puts on the heads, only draws the wire, works, as it were, mechanically, like a machine; he remains half-trained, does not become a master: his labor cannot satisfy him, it can only *fatigue* him. His labor is nothing by itself, has no object in itself, is nothing complete in itself; he labors only into another's hands, and is used (exploited) by this other. For this laborer in another's service there is no *enjoyment of a cultivated mind*, at most, crude amusements: *culture*,

you see, is barred against him."[26]

The "working class" is just that: the caste of people barred from cultural expression and forced to perform menial tasks. While you'd be hard pressed to find a factory in these times, the dark mills of Customer Service are no different: we are forced to abandon our true selves for a crafted personality made by someone else, the lives we sell for pennies on the dollar filled with fake smiles and kiss-assery. This industry is the life-blood of American capitalism; co-owning the work place is merely engaging in self-exploitation. What's a "living wage" if it's only gained by prostrating yourself before every customer, dutifully crushing the competition, and spending years of your life performing the most basic of tasks? Is that the "revolution" you want to fight for? Kill for? DIE FOR? A collectively managed GULAG?

The old ideologies have no place in this century. We desire to be neither good citizens nor good workers, but something far grander: to live lives of our own value, of our own choosing; lives of art, of creativity, of spirit summoning and esoteric secrets! We have touched the very edges of reality, glimpsed into pools only spoken about in legends, spoken with things that have no bodies. And yet we are told that we amount to only our citizenry or our labor? That the banal existence that flickers on our televisions or Soviet newsreels is an ideal to strive for?

No occultist can brook such insolence, no pagan take such thinking seriously. We have a visceral knowledge that there is more to life than the simple machinations of politicians, union leaders, or businessman! Let us find a new flag to unite under, each one a color of our OWN choosing. Let us find and craft a new ideal!

Independently yet interconnected the magic-wielders are waking up. At altars all across this land tears are shed for the fallen and rage fills throbbing hearts. All across the globe the words "something must be done" are uttered. The empty churches of Ideology

---

24   *Ibid.* pg 109
25   *Ibid.* pg 110
26   *Ibid.* pg 110

hear this, feel this, and quiver at the thought of new *adherents, parish-members, and possessed sevites.*

But this a unique moment, unparalleled in human history. The Witches and Wizards are beginning to mobilize alongside other struggles but also amongst themselves. There is no road map here, no manual; no one but yourself can tell you what a magical revolt looks like.

So why ask the decaying species of yesteryear?

The force to evolve, to grow, to further develop; I hold this is the prime motivator of life, not a mere will to survive! The tree seeks to grow its roots, the Kudzu vine seeks to devour the forest, the iguana to grow in size as far as its environment will allow. This Will to Manifest is the prime motivator. So too it exists in people: we work to cultivate or explore our true passions in our leisure, we seek to indulge and cultivate the inner drives and gifts that give us meaning and purpose. This is not the pursuit of perfection per se but a pursuit of greatness and fulfilment.

To each person it is unique, individual. Some of us are painters, singers, and dancers; some of us are builders, crafters, and innovators; some of us work with the elements, some of us call up the Dead, some bind Goetic demons in Triangles of the Art. In cultures and practices so beautifully multifaceted why force one another into desires and ideologies that would rob us of that very uniqueness? Why must you or I be limited, be valued only as much as we can match the prescriptions of a dead century? Are we not dreamers, artists, lovers, and fighters? Are we not as multiplicitous as the very Spirit World we interact with? Then let us NOT become mere SCAFFOLDING, a mere STAIRWAY, soully SACRIFICES for ideological SPOOKS! Let us become Aristocrats of Spirit, who *"should not regard (ourselves) as a function either of the kingship or the commonwealth, but as the SIGNIFICANCE and highest justification thereof"*[27]

It is time for a new politics, a new ideal! It is time for something breathtaking, wild, and unique. Let us be Free Spirits beholden to nothing but ourselves, let us no longer repeat the same tired cantrips of liberation our forebears have handed us!

Forward into a new age, Comrades, ever forward! Abandon the failures of the past in favor of something wholly our own! Let us make our mark on history!

27   Friedrich Nietzsche, *Beyond Good and Evil*, p97

Dr Bones

Dr. Bones is a 9 year practitioner of the Southern occult tradition known as Conjure, Rootwork, and Hoodoo. A skilled card-reader and Spiritworker, Dr. Bones has undertaken all aspects of the work, both benevolent and malefic. Politically he holds the Anarchist line that "Individuality can only flourish where equality of access to the conditions of existence is the social reality. This equality of access is Communism." He resides in the insane State of Florida with his loving wife, a herd of cats, and a house full of spirits. He can be reached through facebook.com/theconjurehouse.

THE FIRE IS HERE

Heathen Chinese

In November 2015, five people protesting the police killing of Jamar Clark, a 24-year-old black man, were shot and injured by a group of white men in Minneapolis.[28] The same week, a candidate for the United States Presidency told the press that a database for all Muslims is "certainly something we should start thinking about."[29] When asked the difference between such an idea and Nazi Germany's registration of Jews and other minorities, his only reply was, "You tell me, you tell me. Why don't you tell me." The same candidate's white supporters physically attacked a black heckler at a rally; the candidate stated in an interview, "Maybe he should have been roughed up."[30] In Greece, the neo-fascist political party Golden Dawn, which has no relation to the occult organization, became the third leading party in the country by winning 7% of the vote in the elections in September 2015, approximately 500,000 votes.[31]

What do Pagans and Polytheists see when they read the news, when they look at history? Do they see deviations from an inevitable progressive march from animism and polytheism to monotheism to atheism, from savagery to barbarism to civilization? Or do they see the snake of the ouroboros choking on its own tail time and time again? Do they see what Walter Benjamin described in 1940—what the Angel of History sees? "Where we see the appearance of a chain of events, he sees one single catastrophe, which unceasingly piles rubble on top of rubble and hurls it before his feet."[32] Or as Rhyd Wildermuth wrote, "History doesn't really 'repeat itself,' *but it's full of repeating forms.*"[33]

Benjamin, looking at the current events of his own time, wrote that those who viewed the rise of fascism as a regression from some sort of historically-ordained "progress" only hindered the struggle against it. He wrote, "The astonishment that the things we are experiencing in the 20th century are 'still' possible is by no means philosophical. It is not the beginning of knowledge, unless it would be the knowledge that the conception of history on which it rests is untenable."[34]

When the new Canadian Prime Minister Justin Trudeau explained the demographics of his newly-appointed Cabinet by saying "Because it's 2015,"[35] he displayed the same kind of historical blindness that Benjamin critiques. Have the Laws of History decreed that sexism, racism and fascism are not possible in 2015, that they

---

28 http://www.nytimes.com/2015/11/25/us/minneapolisshootingprotestpolicejamarclark.html
29 http://www.politifact.com/truthometer/article/2015/nov/24/donaldtrumpscommentsdatabase-americanmuslims/
30 http://www.cnn.com/2015/11/22/politics/donaldtrumpblacklivesmatterprotesterconfrontation/
31 http://www.theguardian.com/world/2015/sep/21/neofascistgreekpartyelectiongoldendawnthird-place
32 Benjamin IX.
33 http://godsandradicals.org/2015/11/24/editorialagainstauthorityagainstterror/
34 Benjamin VIII.
35 http://www.huffingtonpost.ca/2015/11/05/justintrudeausbecauseits2015commentgets-internationalmediaattention_n_8480104.html

are mere fossils from the past? Should we greet fascism's continuity and its re-emergence with astonishment? *Or with preparedness?*

In a fragment from *The Arcades Project,* Benjamin suggested an alternate conception of history. "Marx says that revolutions are the locomotives of world history. But the situation may be quite different. Perhaps revolutions are not the train ride, but the human race grabbing for the emergency brake."[36] Can you hear the reverberating echo of the final prophecy of the Morrígan at the *Second Battle of Mag Tuired?*

> False judgements of old men.
> False precedents of lawyers,
> Every man a betrayer.
> Every son a reaver.[37]

Or perhaps you hear the last gasps of the Race of Iron described by Hesiod in *Works and Days,* as Aidos (Shame) and Nemesis (Retribution) "with their sweet forms wrapped in white robes, will go from the wide-pathed earth and forsake mankind to join the company of the deathless gods: and bitter sorrows will be left for mortal men, and there will be no help against evil."[38]

An anti-progressive conception of history requires radically different ideas about death and ancestry as well. Pagans and Polytheists tend to think about these ideas frequently anyway[39], and what's more, to live them, to embody them, to experience them directly. These ideas are powerful and dangerous, as can be seen by the popularity of Julius Evola among fascists.

From an anti-racist and anti-fascist position, however, we can claim James Baldwin as an Ancestor and Prophet who spoke about these same ideas with refreshing clarity.

Tragedy

In his 1963 book *The Fire Next Time,* Baldwin wrote that the veneer of politics is used by white Americans to conceal the inescapable fact of death:

> Behind what we think of as the Russian menace lies what we do not wish to face, and what white Americans do not face when they regard a Negro: reality—the fact that life is tragic. Life is tragic simply because the earth turns and the sun inexorably rises and sets, and one day, for each of us, the sun will go down for the last, last time.[40]

The word "tragic," of course, traces its etymology back to worship of Dionysos in ancient Greece, to the views of fate and limited human agency put forth by ancient playwrights such as Aeschylus, Sophocles and Euripides. The philosopher Albert Camus defined the "tragic" condition as being characterized not just by death and absurdity, but by self-awareness of one's situation: "The workman of today works everyday in his life at the same tasks, and his fate is no less absurd. But it is tragic only at the rare moments when it becomes conscious."[41]

The awareness and acceptance of the inevitability of death can be seen in many different cultures, in many different traditions and texts. For example, in Homer's *Iliad:*

> As is the generation of leaves, so is that of humanity.

An anti-progressive conception of history requires radically different ideas about death and ancestry

---

36 http://www.yorku.ca/huma1650/Kazis.html
37 Section 167. http://www.sacredtexts.com/neu/cmt/cmteng.htm
38 170201. http://www.sacredtexts.com/cla/hesiod/works.htm
39 https://houndofthecailleach.wordpress.com/2015/10/28/deathsgrossempowerment/
40 Baldwin, *The Fire Next Time,* p 90.
41 http://dbanach.com/sisyphus.htm

The wind scatters the leaves on the ground, but the live timber
burgeons with leaves again in the season of spring returning.
So one generation of men will grow while another dies.[42]

Or in Óinn's words in the *Hávamál*:

Cattle die,
kindred die,
we ourselves also die;
but I know one thing
that never dies,
judgement on each one dead[43]

These themes of successive generations and enduring judgement shall return later in this essay. But first, we must look at the conclusions Baldwin draws from this basic fact. Far from despair, Baldwin exhorts his readers toward an ethic of celebration and passion and responsibility. His words read like the invocation of the Descendants that they are:

It seems to me that one ought to rejoice in the fact of death—ought to decide, indeed, to *earn* one's death by confronting with passion the conundrum of life. One is responsible to life: it is the small beacon in that terrifying darkness from which we come and to which we shall return. One must negotiate this passage as nobly as possible, for the sake of those who are coming after us.[44]

Baldwin sees white Americans' collective willful refusal to acknowledge and "earn" their deaths as the underlying fear that dominates race relations in America: "But white Americans do not believe in death, and this is why the darkness of my skin so intimidates them. And this is also why the presence of the Negro in this country can bring about its destruction."[45] In other words, he speaks of the need to acknowledge the mortality of an entire country or civilization, not just of the individuals within its power structure.

The concept of "race," after all, is ultimately tied to a question of power, an attempt to guarantee a certain societal and cosmological order. The link between the fear of death and the desire for control can be seen in texts as ancient as the *Epic of Gilgamesh*, where the powerful king of Uruk searches for the plant of immortality, only to have it stolen by a serpent as he slept. Power, Baldwin reminds us, is in fact inherently unstable, even though many people think that it is a guarantor of stability:

It is the responsibility of free men to trust and to celebrate what is constant—birth, struggle, and death are constant, and so is love, though we may not always think so—and to apprehend the nature of change, to be able and willing to change. I speak of change not on the surface but in the depths—change in the sense of renewal.

But renewal becomes impossible if one supposes things to be constant that are not—safety, for example, or money, or power. One clings then to chimeras, by which one can only be betrayed, and the entire hope—the entire possibility—of freedom disappears.[46]

> Far from despair, Baldwin exhorts his readers toward an ethic of celebration and passion and responsibility.

---

42   6.146150, trans. Lattimore.
43   Section 77. http://www.heathenhof.com/benjamin-thorpeshavamal/
44   Baldwin *The Fire Next Time*, p 90.

45   Ibid.
46   Ibid. p9091.

Walter Benjamin might say that the possibility of freedom has in fact been betrayed time and time again throughout the history of class-stratified societies, and that "progress" is yet another "chimera." And in the 7th century BCE, Semonides of Argos wrote of the folly of clinging to false hopes, which are always projected into the uncertain future:

> There is no mortal who does not believe that
>   next year
> he will arrive as a friend to Wealth and
>   material goods.
> But one man is first overtaken by hated old age
> before he reaches his goal. Other men
>   are destroyed
> by wretched disease. Others, overcome by War,
> Hades sends down under the black earth.[47]

Ancestors

Death, however, is constant. And so too are the dead, and the ancestors. In a 1971 conversation with the anthropologist Margaret Mead, Baldwin described the experience of drawing upon the strength and legacy of one's ancestors, a feeling that is difficult to define but which can be recognized by anyone who has experienced it:

> *This notion of fame—or infamy, or any other type of experience—being passed down a line of descent is important.*

Baldwin: One's ancestors have given one something, just the same. It is something difficult to get at. You know it when you are in trouble, in real trouble [...] It is not exactly that you hear a voice. It's just that you pull yourself together to confront whatever it is according to some principle which does not exactly exist in your memory but which has been given to you.

Mead: In the name of your ancestors.[48]

Baldwin made clear that when he speaks of ancestors, he is speaking not only of those ancestors who are biologically related, "Let us say I can claim Frederick Douglass as one of my ancestors. I am very proud of him because I think he was a great man and in some way handed something down: his indignation was handed down; his clarity was handed down."[49] The key concept, then, is that he "handed something down," something that future generations can draw upon.

Mead responded, "We have a term for this in anthropology: mythical ancestors. [...] They are spiritual and mental ancestors, they're not biological ancestors, but they are terribly important."[50] The concept is familiar to many Pagans and Polytheists, many of whom have their own terms for these types of ancestors as well: ancestors of spirit, ancestors of tradition, the Mighty Dead. And in ancient Greece, the war dead as well as cult heroes were honored by entire cities, not just by their immediate families. Tyrtaeus of Sparta wrote of the honors due to both warriors who died in battle and to their descendants:

> This man they lament, young and old alike,
> the whole city is affected with a
>   painful longing
> and his tomb and children are
>   conspicuous for fame
>   among men,
> and his children's children and
>   race thereafter.
> Never are his noble fame and his name forgotten,
> but he is immortal, though lying under the earth.[51]

---

47   Trans. Donald Mastronarde.
48   Baldwin, *Rap on Race*.
49   Ibid.
50   Ibid.
51   Trans. M.L. West.

This notion of fame—or infamy, or any other type of experience—being passed down a line of descent is important. This can particularly be seen when Baldwin discusses his relationship with Christianity. He was a Christian preacher in his youth, but left the church after three and a half years. He framed his relationship to Christianity as one of personally "being there"—or not—in certain historical situations:

Baldwin: I wasn't there among the early Christians in the Middle East.
Mead: That's right.
Baldwin: But I was on those cattle boats which brought me here, brought me here in the name of Jesus Christ. [...]
Mead: They did not bring you here in the name of Jesus Christ! That is a perversion.
Baldwin: One of the boats was called "The Good Ship Jesus."[52]

What did Baldwin mean when he said "he was there?" He didn't mean reincarnation of an isolated individual soul. He seems to have meant a certain type of ancestral experience, a certain collapsing of time, an expanded definition of the self, and most importantly, the undeniable and ongoing impact of history on the present. "By the time I was five," he said, he had been "handed down" his ancestors' suffering not just by genetic descent but by his first-hand experience of that history continuing to play itself out:

Baldwin: I had to accept that I was on a slave boat once.
Mead: No.
Baldwin: But I was.
Mead: Wait, you were not. Look, you don't believe in reincarnation?
Baldwin: But my whole life was defined by my history [...] by the time I was five by the history written on my brow.[53]

52   Baldwin, *Rap on Race*.
53   Ibid.

In his 1940 *Dusk of Dawn*, W.E.B. Du Bois similarly called skin color a "badge" of "a common history," "a common disaster" and "one long memory." Du Bois wrote that this badge symbolized an experience shared over time and space:

Now we see the idea of taking responsibility for history

The physical bond is least and the badge of color relatively unimportant save as a badge; the real essence of this kinship is its social heritage of slavery; the discrimination and insult; and this heritage binds together not simply the children of Africa, but extends through yellow Asia and into the South Seas.[54]

Though his life was "defined" by it since he was five years old, Baldwin still spoke of having to "accept" that history. And what happens when people are unable or unwilling accept their histories? In the words of Walter Benjamin, "not even the dead will be safe from the enemy, if he is victorious. And this enemy has not ceased to be victorious."[55]

At the same time, however, Benjamin wrote that "fine and spiritual" qualities are present in the class struggle "as confidence, as courage, as humor, as cunning, as steadfastness," and that "they will, ever and anon, call every victory which has ever been won by the rulers into question."[56] Similarly, in *The Fire Next Time*, Baldwin described the black children who walked through hostile crowds to newly-integrated schools as "improbable aristocrats" possessed of true nobility of spirit. He wrote:

The Negro boys and girls who are facing mobs

54   33.
55   Benjamin VI.
56   Ibid. IV.

today come out of a long line of improbable aristocrats—the only genuine aristocrats this country has produced. I say "this country" because their frame of reference was totally American. They were hewing out of the mountain of white supremacy the stone of their individuality.[57]

Responsibility

Baldwin's ideas about "accepting" his history are closely related to his ideas about responsibility. We have seen Baldwin's call to be "responsible to life." Now we see the idea of taking responsibility for history, and for the failures of the present moment. Responsibility is often conflated with guilt, but is in fact a different concept. In his conversation with Mead, Baldwin not only identified himself with the slave on the boat, but with the Africans who sold other Africans to Europeans as well:

Baldwin: I'm not guiltless, either. I sold my brothers or my sisters—
Mead: When did you?
Baldwin: Oh, a thousand years ago, it doesn't make any difference.[58]

Ironically but tellingly, Baldwin begins *The Fire Next Time* with an epigraph from Rudyard Kipling, which was originally intended to be a "measured" encouragement of U.S. imperialism in the Philippines. But subsequently it was used by Baldwin to call for a true reckoning, a true judgement:

Take up the White Man's burden
Ye dare not stoop to less
Nor call too loud on Freedom
To cloak your weariness;
By all ye cry or whisper,
By all ye leave or do,
The silent, sullen peoples
Shall weigh your Gods and you.[59]

Taken as a justification for colonization, the "White Man's burden" is a disgusting lie. Taken as a commentary on collective responsibility, however, it bears further thought. In his conversation with Mead, Baldwin asked, "How does a civilization distinguish from an individual? It's a loaded question."[60]

Enlightenment thought has led to the glorification of the rational individual. In Benjamin and Baldwin, however, we find traces of older views of the relationship between the individual and society. Michael Löwy, for example, called Benjamin "a prophet; not like someone who tries to see the future, like a Greek oracle, but in the Old Testament sense: that is, one who calls the people's attention to future dangers."[61] Baldwin willingly adopted the same term for himself:

Mead: You're being an Old Testament person.
Baldwin: Prophet.
Mead: You're taking an Old Testament position, that the sins of the fathers are visited on their children.
Baldwin: They are.[62]

This position, though, is far from unique to the Old Testament. For example, the Athenian lawmaker Solon wrote in his hymn "To the Muses" that Zeus's punishment for greed and injustice could be intergenerational as well:

Such is the vengeance
    of Zeus. [...]
One man pays the price
    at once, another
    later on. For those

57 Baldwin, *The Fire Next Time*.
58 Baldwin, *Rap on Race*.
59 Baldwin, *The Fire Next Time*.
60 Baldwin, *Rap on Race*.
61 http://www.walterbenjaminportbou.cat/sites/all/files/2010_Loewy_ANG.pdf
62 Baldwin, *Rap on Race*

who escape
In themselves, and gods'
approaching doom
does not
reach them,
It comes in any case
thereafter.
Innocents pay the price,
Either their children or their
later descendants.[63]

Similarly, Herodotus relates that when Gyges usurped the kingdom of Lydia, the Delphic Oracle of Apollon predicted "that the Heraclids would have their revenge on Gyges in the fifth generation: a prophecy to which neither the Lydians nor their kings paid any attention, until it was actually fulfilled," in the reign of Croesus.[64] And a Chinese prayer to Guan Di warns that those who "entice others to do evil, and do not even a bit of good" themselves will bring down consequences for their entire family: "Retribution will fall upon them, their sons, and their grandsons."[65]

Baldwin's position, however, is more nuanced. He speaks of the way in which a crime committed once can be committed over and over again, by the act of forgetting, by the act of refusing to accept:

Mead: A crime that was committed a long time ago.

Baldwin: The crime that is committed until it is accepted that it was committed. If you don't accept, if I don't accept whatever it is I have done— [...] I 'm doomed to do it forever. If I don't accept what I have done.[66]

He points out the paradox of an entire system that denies personal responsibility: who is responsible for creating such a system—a system not just political or economic, but a "system of reality?" It can only be "all of us:"

We agreed this morning that guilt and responsibility were not the same thing. But we have to agree, too, that we both have produced, all of us have produced, a system of reality which we cannot in an any way whatever control; **what we call history is perhaps a way of avoiding responsibility for what has happened, is happening, in time.** [emphasis added][67]

And thus, he returns to the importance of a personal ethic, of personal honor:

What I am trying to get at is if any particular discipline—whether it be Christianity, Buddhism or LSD, God forbid—does not become a matter of your personal honor, your private convictions, then it's simply a cloak which you can wear or throw off. If it is not interiorized, as we would say these days, then it really is meaningless.[68]

> Taken as a justification for colonization, the "White Man's burden" is a disgusting lie. Taken as a commentary on collective responsibility, however, it bears further thought.

---

63 Trans. M.L. West.
64 1.13, trans. De Selincourt.
65 https://heathenchinese.wordpress.com/guanshengdijun-prayers/
66 Baldwin, *Rap on Race*.
67 Ibid.
68 Ibid.

THE FIRE IS HERE

Vengeance and Salvation

If the "system of reality" we have constructed lies beyond the responsibility of any one person or organization, if history itself is "a way of avoiding responsibility," what can cut through this Gordian Knot? In *The Fire Next Time,* Baldwin warns of "historical vengeance, a cosmic vengeance." A divine vengeance, an ancestral vengeance:

> The intransigence and ignorance of the white world might make that vengeance inevitable—a vengeance that does not really depend on, and cannot really be executed by, any person or organization, and that cannot be prevented by any police force or army: historical vengeance, a cosmic vengeance, based on the law that we recognize when we say, "Whatever goes up must come down."[69]

Baldwin had already written these words by the time he sat down with Margaret Mead. He had written, too, of the mistake of "clinging to chimeras." And so, Baldwin sought to slay the "chimera" of American self-importance, shocking Mead greatly:

> Baldwin: From my point of view, America does not matter so very much.
> Mead: What does?
> Baldwin: Mexico matters.
> Mead: You think—
> Baldwin: Vietnam matters.
> Mead: You think that Mexico and Vietnam can save the world? I mean for the future?
> Baldwin: I know that we will not.
> Mead: Well, if we don't save it—
> Baldwin: We won't.
> Mead: Jimmy, if we don't save it we will destroy it.
> Baldwin: We won't. My point precisely.
> Mead: And Mexico and Vietnam will have nothing to do with it.
> Baldwin: My point precisely.
> Mead: All right. You are saying, then, the world is going to be destroyed; there is no use doing anything about it?
> Baldwin: No. I don't intend to be passive. But America will not save us.[70]

Like Semonides of Argos, Baldwin accepts the reality of the present without delusion about the future: "The future doesn't exist for me. [...] I am not romantic. I am not at home here and never will be."

Let us, too, take a clear look at the time we find ourselves in. *The Fire Next Time* is couched as a warning of an impending apocalypse, which could perhaps be averted if the "intransigence and ignorance of the white world" are abandoned. But this has not happened. And just as the crime is

> who is responsible for creating such a system—a system not just political or economic, but a "system of reality?" It can only be "all of us."

[69] Baldwin *The Fire Next Time.*

[70] Baldwin, *Rap on Race*

committed anew until it is accepted, so is the destruction of the world an *ongoing process*, not a "future" one.

Let us avoid the pitfall of the Christians who are eternally trying to predict the date of the Rapture, forced to forever re-calculate as the proclaimed date arrives and passes. Time is not linear progress, but cyclical, compressed and eternal. The fire is not coming "next time," it is already here, and it has been here.

And as we began this article with reference to the police shooting of Jamar Clark, so we end it with a final quote from James Baldwin:

I don't care *how* well the cops are educated. I know what their role is in my life, and I will not accept it.[71]

What more needs to be said?

Heathen Chinese

Heathen Chinese is a son of Chinese immigrants living in the San Francisco Bay Area—stolen Ohlone land. He is a multi-tradition polytheist with devotions to Guan Di, Zhao Gong Ming, ancestors, ancestors of and in the land, Hestia, Hermes, Aphrodite, the Matronae, Odin, and warrior/soldier ancestors. He writes at http://heathenchinese.wordpress.com.

71   Ibid.

Bataille and the Dead:
From the Death of the City of Man to Sacred Expenditure

Finnchuill

"Depletion was there from the outset: in the first lump of coal burned, there was energy derived from the destruction of a resource. The fossil fuels, and the electricity, that drive Empire are depletion: if they could not be depleted, burned up, they could not provide energy. Fossil fuel is the passage of time as decay, as petrifaction, the shift from life to death as living things are transformed into valuable and exploitative reserves; it is also the ticking time of the loss of resources, of the limit"

—Allan Stoekl, *Batailles's Peak*

Dark earth, black soil: occluded in night is the grave mound, long forgotten, screened off by the gleaming, shining world of the gas station, the mall, the database. Yet a dark ecology lingers in the underpasses, the back lots; teeming, virulent, ignored by a billion commuters plugged in, disconsciously huffing oil, the black gold.

Depletion

A race fueled by death. We dream it on the big screens, *Mad Max Fury Road,* speeding onto whatever end, a terminus where everyone left has a terminal condition, where no one is left standing—and all in a cloud of literal death; the haze of Beijing, the exhaust of Delhi, the stain of LA's sky. The spectral presence of the dead, of the long buried and now burned dead of primeval green life hanging like a pall, a shroud over the biosphere. The squalid miasma of the sixth super extinction, the death of lemurs, of poison frogs, of city-building corals, the effluvia settling on our skins, clogging the ducts of our souls... All while the motley crowd, glued to screens, does everything possible to avoid thoughts of their own death, of their finitude, as the rich dream of cyber-heavens of downloaded lives and literal evasion of death. One of the new promised toys of distraction is the self-driving Google car, where owners can entertain themselves while Google's algorithms drive their vehicle, even in the fall of peak oil, even in the burn of catastrophic climate change, oblivious.

The thought of French philosopher and writer Georges Bataille (1897-1962) can help reveal the 'limited economy', its role in creating this wasteland that is blighting the entire biosphere, and via an understanding of the 'accursed share', hidden by modernist productive ideology, afford pagans insights into a life beyond utility in a 'general economy' of sacred expenditure, one where the dead (always) await, and animality returns to us.

The modern city is designed for the car, the city that Georges Bataille called the City of Man[72]. The City of Man is the universalist city, the city of the modern, endlessly raising Man up, as the pinnacle of all things. The City of Man is designed for speed, and the City of Man dissolves place in speed and capital. The city becomes pure space in the circuitry of the automobiles; the city of speed has no place for the Dead. This City runs on extreme concentrations of energy. Bataille saw that Marxism, in its focus on the human, overlooked the central role of energy in economics and life itself. Humans may produce, but that is dependent on the amount of en-

[72] The City of Man, a city of the (white) 'man of reason', the inheritor of the Enlightenment and colonialism, who has replaced (the Biblical) God.

A BEAUTIFUL RESISTANCE

ergy that they can utilize, as nature and the social, in Bataille's thought, are at once energy concentrations and expending (waste) (Stoekl, *Bataille's Peak* 32).

Bataille wrote in *The Accursed Share,* "Man's disregard for the material basis of his life still causes him to err in a serious way. Humanity exploits given material resources, but by restricting them as it does to a resolution of the immediate difficulties it encounters (a resolution that it has hastily had to define as an ideal), it assigns to the forces it employs an end which they cannot have" (21). He wrote *The Accursed Share* in the late 1940s, with an understanding that life receives a surfeit of energy (against the grain of western civilization's foundational belief in scarcity) and abundance, of a "Copernican transformation" where, "If a part of wealth is doomed to destruction or at least to unproductive use without any possible profit, it is logical, even *inescapable,* to surrender commodities without return" (AS 25). He calls this a reversal of both economics and ethics. Historically, the increase of wealth and technological advances have been the result not just of human labor but of the discovery/ability to harness increasingly rich concentrated energy sources, going historically from wood to coal to petroleum. "Wealth, in other words, has its origins not just in the productivity of human labor and its ever more sophisticated human refinements, as both the bourgeois and Marxist traditions would argue, but in the energy released from (primarily) fossil fuels through the use of innovative devices" (Stoekl, RBN 256). And the heat keeps rising.

Energy

Since the car runs on the energy of the sun that was long ago gathered by primordial algae and plankton, dead bodies fossilized over the eons transformed into the most energy rich of fuels, let's consider the central role of energy in Bataille's thought. The sun plays a key role in Bataille's cosmos: it is an endless source of energy, and unspeakably generous. "The sun gives without ever receiving. Men were conscious of this long before astrophysics measured that ceaseless prodigality; they saw it ripen the harvest and associated its splendor with the acts of someone who gives without receiving" (*Accursed Share* 29). He goes on to observe that in former times value was given to this glory, but that in our time value is measured by production. So the cosmos is unrestrained in its giving, in its flow, even though humans do not, could not, have the ability to capture most of these flows (but have more than utility can take).

Limits to growth are always imposed, either ecologically in the carrying capacity of land, or ideologically in the completion of a semiotic system: the excess must always be burned off, or plowed under in some way, whether simply by increased warfare, or in sacrificial rounds of excess, or in ideologies via the exclusion into the 'unseen' zones of the unspeakable,

> This 'cursed matter' is "not only matter that is leftover and so can contribute its energy to further growth; it is also matter that is burned off, which leads nowhere beyond itself, and so is dangerous, powerful, sacred.

the unavowable. Such excluded matter Bataille called 'base'. It ultimately cannot be controlled by any system; it is always subversive. While some of this energy can be put into productive work, it is too excessive to control, and it will be more than could ever be put to a utilitarian end. This 'cursed matter' is "not only matter that is leftover and so can contribute its energy to further growth; it is also matter that is burned off, which leads nowhere beyond itself, and so is dangerous, powerful, sacred. Bataille's energy shoots through a charged matter that obtrudes in sacred ritual and erotic 'wounds': the 'share' of energy is not a resulting order but a base disorder" (Stoekl, BP 34). It is not positioned in time in a way that it can be a means to a utility, but remains always its own end.

The (Unproductive) Expenditure

So an organism, a person, or a society comes up against its limits, and the excess, the accursed share, must be expended whether in ritual violence, lavish arts, eroticism with no productive purposes or in catastrophic ruin and endless warfare (as of the American empire). Bataille was much influenced by Marcel Mauss' study of the potlatch[73], and more generally gift economies, in *The Gift: The Form and Reason For Exchange In Archaic Societies*. In his three volume work of an interdisciplinary re-evaluation of political economy, *The Accursed Share*, written in the years following the cataclysm of destruction of World War II and its related atrocities, Bataille sought for a conscious understanding of expenditure, distinguishing an unethical squandering vs. good squandering (the problem inherent in the fact that humans must expend). Humans being at the top of the food chain are massive burners of energy, whether of petroleum, muscle, wind, wood, or meat. They will squander one way or another, but Bataille as an ethicist probed ways that were less destructive than the Protestant-capitalist displacement, which is more or less unconscious, and observed the irony of this system that doesn't give, that holds on, makes everything into a standing reserve, but squanders prolifically in its war machines, and its caterpillar-on-steroids consumption cycles, including radical depletion of the fuel of the system itself.

This is a waste bereft of the beauty of the Northwest Coast potlatch, the throwing of wealth into European lakes in Iron Age rituals of destruction, the Dionysian processions of Ptolemaic Alexandria, or the sacrificial rites of Tenochtitlan, to name but a very few examples. These are not, or are only partially, attached to the world of things, of the world of utility, where everything done is done for a return on investment, as an investment, not as a sacrifice or gift. Bataille terms the utilitarian world a 'restricted economy', while the world of sacrifice without reservation, is that of a 'general economy'. In this 'general economy', where actions are taken without attachment to result, intimacy in the Bataillean sense can occur, a communication where persons are not trapped in the shells of their identities, where the self becomes porous and open to the other, and a continuity between usually discontinuous subjects flows.

The contemporary capitalist order wastes in a qualitatively different manner: things are to be quickly consumed, thus their wastage is not a consumption of intimate destruction, of sacrifice, but the efficient way of discarding in a cycle of continuous overproduction. No one experiences sacred loss in the endless conveyor belt of tiny changes to smartphones that are built so as to make repair nearly impossible; made in China, they then return to China to compose garbage mountains sifted through for usable but toxic materials by children and adults, unprotected by safety gear (Baichwal), people whose marginality is a utility in this heartless cycle

---

73   These competitive giftgiving rites with their destruction of the gifts of the Northwest Coast Indians of the US and Canada were banned under Canadian and US laws in the late 19th centuries, as being barbarically opposed to civilization's capitalist laws of accumulation. *Potlatch* was the name of a Lettrist and Situationist journal of the 1950s.

of commodities and utilitarian waste.

Some have misunderstood Bataille's expenditure as finding realization in capitalist consumption but this is really the opposite of intimacy in Bataille's terms, which is an essential trait of sacrificial expenditure (Stoekl, RBN 271). The same can be said of the extraordinary waste of fossil fuels, those dead forests and algae ponds of the saurian age previously mentioned, all of which occurs in a regime of utility, of production for 'rational' ends of industry and its satisfaction of consumer identities in SUVs, parking lots, and the vast array of goods in the big box stores that now stud the planet.

A prime element in Bataille's investigation was the role of the automobile in the modern city, the universalist City of Man. As a primary component of the City, the car and its endless circuits, its indifference to its surrounds, its exhaustions of dynamism, result in the City's dependence on the fuel, the petroleum that oils the machine, that fuel whose limit can be seen on the horizon (or then again, apparently, it cannot by many). Yet that endless movement and desired speed has long kept the horizon that is also death at bay, beyond consciousness.

Allan Stoekl gives a closer look at the operation of the automobile: "The car runs on fuel. It burns it, it consumes it, and it can only move if the fuel is burnable, if the fuel is finite. The car's universality, and the self on which it depends, are a function of an energy that can be expended and will soon be gone: the car's fall. At the moment of the recognition of the finitude of fuel, the space of the car opens out to another space, the space of another expenditure: that of the walker, dancer, or cyclist in the city; the flaneur, the voyeur, the exhibitionist - the one who lurks under the arch" (BP 185). The arch, this gateway, is also where the prostitute waits; in the ancient city or in many a modern one, a liminal place[74]. Eroticism, in Bataille's view, is an unrestricted expenditure, an opening to the sacred; whereas (modern) sexuality, which is productively invested in ideologies of identity and often literal reproduction of the social order, is the reduction of a closed economy.

Walking is a different regime of expenditure, which puts the walker in intimacy with that which is around. Stoekl writes:

"To burn energy with one's body is grossly inefficient if one has a car at one's disposal. If gas is cheap, as it always has been, and (from the perspective of the official energy experts) evidently always will be, it is inefficient to walk. You needlessly expend time, you incur physical discomfort, you are distracted by inessential things. Movement is choppy, disarticulated; you are constantly reminded of the passage of time and the finite hide of our own body: death. Unfortunately surprises suddenly arise. The world is full of base matter, matter closing with uncontrollable energy: you are confronted with disgusting smells, the vision of dirt, of rotting things in gutters. You are needlessly spending bodily energy, and time, perilously in contact with matter that could just as easily

No one experiences sacred loss in the endless conveyor belt of tiny changes to smartphones that are built so as to make repair nearly impossible

[74] Such as ancient Athenian male and female sex workers, see: James N. Davidson, *Courtesans and Fishcakes*. University of Chicago Press, 2011.

be entirely separated from the movement of a pure awareness, a pure present" (BP 187).

The walker is confronting the modern city through the sacrifice of their energy, in expenditure. The walker may have to cross difficult interchanges, walk where the sidewalk gives out, where the way is paved with shattered glass, where weeds, those unuseful plants, partially curtain a hidden world of feral and dead, and may witness an accident, a crash. Perhaps the mangled mating of two or more cars, as in J. G. Ballard's novel of depletion, *Crash*. This world was designed for the automobile, but its system designed by transportation experts, urban planners and engineers of various varieties is a closed system; much of base matter, vibrantly alive, has escaped it. Here we can talk about the spirits and the dead, especially the dead.

The dead weren't always banished away from the living. The boundaries were permeable. Archaeology in its negotiations with the past pulls back habitations where the skulls and bones of the dead were interred under the living quarters of homes, as in Çatal Hüyük and other archaic Near Eastern settlements, including the beautifully decorated plaster skulls of the Levantine Neolithic[75].

Historian Claude Lecouteux writes of a Europe where Christianity had to work hard to implement a segregation of the living and the dead, a separation that was not that of ancient belief and custom. The dead who had not died well, before their time, violently, with unfinished business, a need for revenge, those who had gotten along poorly when alive, could return as revenants, walking embodied dead, rather than spectral ghosts. Through a lexical archaeology, Lecouteux traces the attempt, eventually more or less successful, to change them into evil demons or other entities that fit into the Church's dualistic moral cosmology. "In short, they cause trouble and create a shock within a Christianized society that has installed a simple redemptive and punitive scheme with three sides: hell, purgatory, and heaven" (144).

Lecouteux states the dead are associated in the Germanic world with the Dumezilian third function[76], the function associated with fertility, fecundity, the production of the land; I think this could be opened up wider in the greater Indo-European context. This brings in mounds, which play a prominent role in Celtic lore, as well as in the Germanic/Norse. This element reveals the integral relationship of the dead with the well-being of the land. Interestingly, in some sagas, burial mounds have such vitality that they remain green in the winter (Lecouteux 184). Lecouteux notes that the dead can control weather, and the dissatisfied ones can bring storms and other inclement conditions (185).

It can be fascinating to contemplate what this might mean to a social order where the dead are frequently banished almost completely from the City of Man, as they were from the city of San Francisco, where they were exiled beyond the borders to a nearby suburban city of the dead (Colma). Or in Los Angeles' famous Forest Lawn Cemetery where traditional tombstones were removed from cemetery design so as to make a 'happy place' for visitors, the signs of

> The dead weren't always banished away from the living.

---

75 Many years ago, I was fortunate to have the experience of traveling in the Indonesian island of Sumba where I was forcefully struck by the villages where the living and dead were integrated, with the houses of the living more or less in a ring around the huge stone tombs of the dead in the center.

76 Georges Dumezil proposed a trifunctional ideology of early IndoEuropean cultures, roughly involving those involved with sovereignty (priest, jurists), the warriors, and those of production (agriculture, pastoral, etc.) as reflected, for example, in the Brahmans, Kshatriya, and Vaishya in Indian tradition.

death erased from view. Of course, where the modern city banishes even the cemetery in an ultimate step, the dead can only reappear elsewhere destructively, as endless zombie narratives suggest.

Yet destruction can lead to the possibility of new community. Bataille said that we must face the horizon of death. I suggest that the dead 'wait' there for us who are willing to cross, even though dread is involved. In terms of our present situation/predicament on this planet, I think facing the horror of what we moderns have wrought unconsciously, or not, in the wreckage of the weave of the vast living communities of life forms, including those of indigenous and othered human communities, can only bring us into a condition of anguish, one that can puncture our sense of discontinuity with the rest of life (and death). Facing and experiencing this horror can create a possibility of future ethical communities.

The going out from the City of Man crosses into waste ground, the cemetery where the vine flourishes among the skulls, out through the gate in festival and into a (lost) world of animal intimacy, in a collapse of utilitarianism in unproductive expenditure, a rupture of hard-shelled subject identities in a world of eroticism, where disheveled maenads[77] move with the dreaming, headless Dionysos (the Acéphale)[78]. We find ourselves without project, among the (other) animals, and the dead with whom we find we are no longer discontinuous. Nothing can be known there, but I see a throng wanders into undefined new possibilities in a rite of communication, opening up new communities[79]. This going out through the gate into intimacy must happen over and over and over.

FINNCHUILL

Finnchuill is a Celtic Polytheist, a fili, a druid, an animist, a Dionysian, and mystes of Antinous. This queer polytheist-at-large blogs at finnchuillsmast.wordpress.com and writes for Air-N-Aithesc, a Celtic Reconstructionist magazine, and is the author of a book of devotional poetry From the Prow of Myth. Finnchuill works as a college educator and is currently living in Hawai'i in a house shared with geckos.

---

77   "...the disheveled animality of the maenads" *The Accursed Share, Vol. II*, 140.
78   The Acéphale is the headless monstrous god/man who represents the loss of instrumental reason in the sacred. Jeremy Biles posits the Acéphale as Dionysus dreaming (see "Does The Acéphale Dream of Headless Sheep" in *Negative Ecstasies*.)
79   Bataille saw community as a throng of undefined possibility.

Millennium

Christopher Scott Thompson

Black birds come screeching through the skies
On winds of war, as waters rise.
And prophets' eyes begin to gleam
Beneath their floating hair. This dream
Of smoke and fire shall end at last!
A whisper rises from the past –
Millennium – as pillars shake
Millennium – as gods awake
Millennium – as flowers bloom
In mouths of corpses, and the tomb
Springs open to reveal the Host
Arranged for battle, ghost by ghost,
With banners flapping, black and red.
Millennium – "We are the dead
Who rose with Spartacus and fell,
Who sang *John Ball Has Rung Your Bell*,
Who marched with pitchforks on Versailles,
And those who answered Boukman's cry,
Who rode with Makhno in Ukraine,
And those who died defending Spain.
We are the dead of all the earth
Who died to bring this day to birth.
The dead who dreamed another world
Have come to you with flags unfurled.
The burning wheels and turning gears
Have come around. The end is near.
Our work remains undone. But you
(Millennium!) shall see it through.
So take your mental spear, and go!
Cast down all thrones. Let forests grow
Where burning mills once filled the sky
With smoke and flame. Let empires die,
Till none is slave and none is king.
Then heal. Then build. Then sing."

A BEAUTIFUL RESISTANCE

Christopher Scott Thompson

Christopher Scott Thompson is a founder of Clann Bhride: The Children of Brighid, a writer for Gods & Radicals, and a historical swordsmanship instructor. Chris was active with Occupy St Paul and Occupy Minneapolis. He lives in Portland, Maine, with his wife and two daughters.

About the Artists

Lorna Smithers,
Hawthorn beside the river Ribble,
Photography

Dutch Pagan
Blood Bond
Black ink and dragonblood ink on paper.

Dutch Pagan (just call her Yv) enjoys a healthy mix of paganism, art, nature, witchcraft, folklore and history which she combines in arts, crafts, and writings. Find her on Facebook, Twitter, and Tumblr.

Pegi Eyers
Turtle Moon
Acrylic on canvas.

Loïs Cordelia
Mythology and Folklore of the British Isles
Scalpel paper-cut.

Loïs Cordelia (born 1982, Ipswich) is a prolific UK artist and illustrator in cut-paper, acrylics and mixed media. She works in diverse styles, ranging from intricate scalpel paper-cut designs to energetic acrylic speed-painting. Since 1999, she has been a studio assistant to children's illustrator Jan Pienkowski (born 1936, Warsaw), and holds a first level Honours degree in Arabic from the University of Edinburgh. Loïs' website includes a comprehensive portfolio and a dynamic record of her busy schedule of exhibitions, live art demos, workshops, talks, and other events. www.LoisCordelia.com.

Brianna Bliss
Earth Mound Mother, Sustain-her of Life
Digital Photography Collage

Brianna Bliss is a student of archetypal language; writer, poet, artist and submitted vessel for divine intervention. She promotes Verbal Alchemy, that is, that words are magick and we heal through expression of all our parts. For pleasure she reads, dances, explodes on a page, blows glass, and explores what she can of the web of life and its synchronicities. You can view works by her alter-ego, the raw B. Wilder, at www.verbal-alchemy.com.

Hanne T. Fisker

Walking the Wall, By the Old Stone, The Holy Grove, Carrifran Wildwood, Constellations of Dew, The High Hills
Photography

Gordon MacLellan

Toadstools and **Water Boggart**
Photography of Environmental Art.

Runic John

Soulfood

Mixed media acrylic and acrylic pen painted on board

Runic John is an Author, Artist, Heathen, Shaman and Rune worker. His recent book Up and Down the Tree: Exploring the Nine Worlds of Yggdrasil has received much acclaim in Heathen and Shamanic circles alike. His Artwork has been exhibited Nationally and internationally beside such well known contemporary Artists as Tracey Emin and Billy Childish. When not traversing the nine worlds or in his studio making Art, Runic can be found stomping to the sound of Psytrance in festival fields worldwide. You can check out his work on facebook: https://www.facebook.com/Runic-John-Artist-925056017527740/?ref=hl or here: https://www.artfinder.com/runicjohn.

Li Pallas

Cover and Layout Design

Born to aetheist divorcées in suburban New York, Li Pallas formed an existential sense of otherworldliness. She sees prophecy as a series of complex narratives used to interpret the human condition, illuminating the trappings of corporeal melodrama and moving us towards ethical choice. She finds meaning in talking to strangers in installations she invents, creates fine art print media as an affront to systemic narcissism, writes theory on aesthetics and intersectional justice, and moonlights as a book designer at Gods & Radicals.   www.lipallaslovesyou.com

THE FIRE IS HERE

WORKS CITED

Yvonne Aburrow: Only Connect

Chas S. Clifton, *Her Hidden Children: The Rise of Wicca and Paganism in America*, 2006, Pagan Studies Series, Altamira Press

Starhawk, *Truth or Dare: Encounters with Power, Authority and Mystery*, 1988, San Francisco, HarperSanFrancisco), http://starhawk.org/writing/books/truth-or-dare/

Chris Stokel-Walker, A Quick Chat With The Busker Who Sang "F*ck Off Back To Eton" At David Cameron – 2015, *Buzzfeed* http://www.buzzfeed.com/chrisstokelwalker/the-fuck-off-back-to-eton-busker-is-on-a-train-t-17b68

Rhyd Wildermuth: We Are The Rude

Silvia Federici, *Caliban and the Witch*, 2004 Autonomedia

Hannah Arendt, *The Origins of Totalitarianism*, 1951 Shocken Books

Marian T. Horvat (translator), *Catholic Manual of Civility*, English edition 2008

Kadmus: Of Worlding

Erik Havlock, *Preface to Plato*, 1982, Belknap Press

Harold Bloom, *Homer's Iliad: Modern Critical Interpretations*, 2006, Chelsea House Publications

Hitakonanu'Laxk, *The Grandfathers Speak: Native American Folk Tales of the Lenape People*, 1993, Interlink Pub Group

Kevin Robb, *Language and Thought in Early Greek Philosophy*, 1983, Open Court Publishing Company

Paul Feyerabend, *Farewell to Reason*, 1988, Verso

Dr Bones: The Sui Generis Sermon

Friedrich Nietzsche, *Beyond Good and Evil*, 2014, Millennium Publications,

Max Stirner, *The Ego and His Own*, The Case of the Individual Against Authority, 2014, Verso

Heathen Chinese: The Fire Is Here

James Baldwin, *The Fire Next Time*, 1963, New York: The Dial Press

James Baldwin and Margaret Mead, *A Rap On Race*, 1971 Philadelphia: J.B. Lippincott Company

Walter Benjamin, "On the Concept of History," 1940, https://www.marxists.org/reference/archive/benjamin/1940/history.htm

Finnchuill: Bataille And The Dead

Allan Stoekl, *Bataille's Peak: Energy, Religion, And Postsustainability*, 2007, Minneapolis: University of Minnesota Press

---. "Excess and Depletion: Bataille's Surprisingly Ethical Model of Expenditure", *Reading Bataille Now*, 2007, Ed. Winnubst. Print.

Claude Lecoteux *The Return of the Dead: Ghosts, Ancestors, and the Transparent Veil of the Pagan Mind*, 2009, Trans. Jon E. Graham. Rochester, VT: Inner Traditions

Georges Bataille, *The Accursed Share*, 1991, Vol. I. Trans. Robert Hurley. NY: Zone Books

---. *The Accursed Share. Vols. II & III*, 1993, Trans. Robert Hurley. NY: Zone

Jeremy Biles and Kent L. Brintnall, *Negative Ecstasies: Georges Bataille and the Study of Religion*, 2015, NY: Fordham University Press

Jennifer Baichwal with Edward Burtynsky. *Manufactured Landscapes*. 2006. Film.

Shannon Winnubst, ed. *Reading Bataille Now*, 2007, Bloomington & Indianapolis: Indiana University Press

A BEAUTIFUL RESISTANCE

www.ingramcontent.com/pod-product-compliance
Lightning Source LLC
Chambersburg PA
CBHW051611030426